North Wales Walking on the level

Norman and June Buckley

2nd Edition © Norman and June Buckley, 2010

1st edition published 2001

Published by Sigma Leisure – an imprint of
Sigma Press, Stobart House, Pontyclerc, Penybanc Road
Ammanford, Carmarthenshire SA18 3HP

British Library Cataloguing in Publication Data

A CIP record for this book is available from the British Library

ISBN: 978-1-85058-863-4

Typesetting and Design by: Sigma Press, Ammanford, Carms

Maps: © Bute Cartographics

Photographs: © June Buckley

Cover photographs: © Norman and June Buckley
Main picture: Conwy Estuary
Left to right: Ffestiniog Railway, Morfa Nefyn, Ruined chapel near Moelfre, Abersoch harbour

Printed by: Cromwell Group, Trowbridge, Wiltshire

Disclaimer: The information in this book is given in good faith and is believed to be correct at the time of publication. Care should always be taken when walking in hill country. Where appropriate, attention has been drawn to matters of safety. The author and publisher cannot take responsibility for any accidents or injury incurred whilst following these walks. Only you can judge your own fitness, competence and experience. Do not rely solely on sketch maps for navigation: we strongly recommend the use of appropriate Ordnance Survey (or equivalent) maps.

Preface

At last – the long-awaited companion to the two Lake District, the Yorkshire Dales and the Peak District level walking books. Perhaps this is the ultimate challenge in England and Wales – to guide walkers among the high, uncompromisingly rugged, mountains of Snowdonia, the adjacent hills and the less demanding countryside of Anglesey, in all cases without actually climbing those hills and mountains, and without ascents which are too demanding either in terms of length or steepness.

It is apparent that the earlier books have achieved their objective and have encouraged walkers who do not climb mountains or high hills to visit the most beautiful parts of their respective areas.

For those coming to these books for the first time, here is a brief outline of the 'level walks' philosophy. First and foremost, the term 'level' must not be taken literally; very few walks could meet this absolute criterion over a distance of more then a few metres. Rather, it indicates that in selecting and trying out possible routes for inclusion, the author's first consideration is the ascent, both in total and in the length and/or steepness of individual uphill sections within that total. The belief is that many people enjoy walking among the hills and great mountains but, for a variety of reasons, are not able or do not wish to climb significantly. Age and/or disability, mistrust of high and wild places, doubts about safe return routes and the presence of young children are only some of the reasons why books of gentle walks, with reliable directions, are needed.

Good footpaths and bridleways are used wherever practicable, with quiet lanes and minor roads being included where they are essential for the completion of a circuit. Just a glance at the introductory material for each walk is sufficient to make a decision on the suitability of that walk for any person or group on any particular occasion. The same introduction also gathers together potentially useful information on refreshments, car parking, maps and the features to be seen along the way. As walking speeds are very variable, likely times for a walk are not given; many walkers find that two miles per hour applied to the distance will work out quite accurately, allowing some time for view and photography stops, but do add extra time for a picnic.

Coupled with the sketch maps, the detailed route directions will suffice to guide walkers, with a reliable return to the starting place. Nevertheless, the use of a large scale (1:25,000) map is highly recommended, adding a great deal to the appreciation of the landscape. Snowdonia and Anglesey are often wet and even good paths can become impromptu streams, whilst farmland suffers from churning by livestock. Walking boots are, therefore, the only reliable all-weather footwear.

Acknowledgement

In preparing the material for this book, the author acknowledges the shared enthusiasm and the invaluable support of his wife June, also the companionship and local knowledge of Joan and Ray Dixon.

Contents

Walk 1: The Great Orme, Llandudno

A lovely walk giving a rare opportunity to walk at a moderately high level yet with minimum rise and fall. This circuit of the Great Orme's Head has wonderful views of great expanses of sea and mountains.

Distance	4¼ km (2¾ miles)
Ascent	70m (230ft) No steep ascents
Maps	Ordnance Survey Explorer OL17, Snowdon and Conwy Valley, 1:25,000 Ordnance Survey Landranger 115, Snowdon, 1:50,000
Start/Parking	Informal parking area on grass, above St Tudno's Church at the point where a farm track leaves the little road. From the town, take the steep road to Gt. Orme's Head turning right at the junction about 100 metres before the entrance to the copper mine visitor attraction. Grid reference 769836
Refreshments:	At visitor complex on hill summit. Tea shop at Copper Mine

About the Area

Llandudno is a large town by North Wales standards, bustling even out of the holiday season, and very busy indeed when droves of holidaymakers add to the resident population. It has the rare distinction of having two sea fronts, one facing west to Conwy Bay, whilst the main beach and the town centre are on the east side of the neck of flat land which connects the 'mainland' with the huge mound of the Great Orme.

Many centuries ago this land was under water and the Orme was an impressive island, with limestone pavements and other rock features among abundant gorse.

Great Orme tramway

The town has museums, art gallery, gardens and other attractions appropriate to a large resort. The Great Orme has also, inevitably, had visitor attractions added to its scenic interest. In late Victorian times a tramway was constructed from town to summit and a hotel, now converted into a visitor complex including restaurant and other catering, was built at the summit. (207m - 679ft). Copper mines originating in the Bronze Age have been developed and opened for visitors and there is a country park, with visitor centre. In addition to the tramway there is a more recent cable car service from close to the pier to the summit.

Many walkers may prefer to walk round the Orme out of the holiday season, when the facilities are closed and the wind blows hard from the Irish Sea

The Walk

Leave the parking area along the farm access trackway, broad and easy.

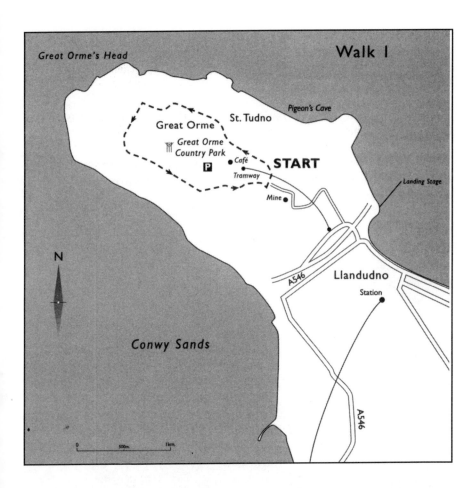

Below, to the right, is St. Tudno's Church, with its huge burial ground. Above, to the left, are the summit buildings and Parc Farm, with its grazing land enclosed by a substantial stone wall.

The track bends to the left to stay close to the wall, rising very gently, passing a small area of limestone pavement. Bend to the left again to stay by the wall and make the longest ascent of the circuit, on short grass,

At the top of the rise the views open up to the west with hills and mountains most attractively displayed across Conwy Bay.

Along this section of the walk there are several nature trail signposts; the unerring navigational guide is the farm wall. At the corner of the wall, where it turns sharply upwards, bear half left to rise fairly gently to the Great Orme access road.

Turn right, along the roadside, as far as the junction opposite the Great Orme Mine.

Turn left at the junction, cross the tramway lines, pass under the cable way and follow the minor road back to the parking area.

On the Great Orme, Llandudno

Walk 2: Conwy

A circular walk which combines the attraction of the historic little town of Conwy, including the quay, with the surrounding countryside.

Distance	5 km (3 miles)
Ascent	65m (213ft), mostly on hard surface, at reasonable gradients
Underfoot	No difficulties. One ladder stile
Maps	Ordnance Survey Explorer OL17 Snowdon and the Conwy Valley, 1:25,000 Ordnance Survey Landranger 115, Snowdon, 1:50,000
Start/Parking	Large pay and display car park, with public conveniences, situated immediately outside the town wall, accessed from the B5106, Trefriw, road. Grid reference 782774
Refreshments:	Wide choice in Conwy

About the Area

Famous as the site of one of the great castles built by King Edward I to subdue the Welsh, Conwy's history over the centuries is both rich and diverse. The massive structure of the castle is joined by an equally impressive town wall, one of the best surviving examples in Europe, protecting a rich array of buildings squeezed between wall and estuary. The walk along the top of the western section of this wall provides a gallery from which the views, near and far, are magnificent.

Within this compact town are several fine and historic buildings. Finest of all is Plas Mawr, a gabled mansion built in 1576 by an Elizabethan adventurer, now beautifully restored inside and out. Even older is the 14th century Aberconwy House, with overhanging upper story, now cared for by the National Trust, housing a shop and Conwy

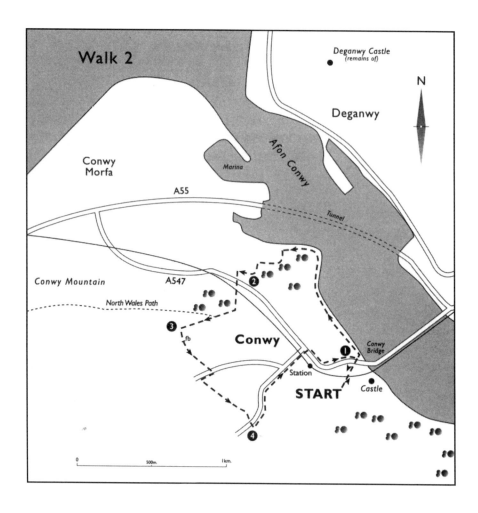

exhibition. On a different level, in more ways than one, is the claimed smallest house in Britain, a mid Victorian structure on the Quay just 122 inches in height and 72 inches in width, open to visitors in season.

The town had associations with Welsh princes; the Cistercian Conwy Abbey was founded by Llewellyn the Great. The monks were dispersed by Edward I, who had a new church, St. Mary's, constructed on the site. For centuries a small port, Conwy still has a minor fishing industry operating from the attractive quay. Close by the quay, the importance of the river crossing is emphasised by the number of bridges. Pride of place goes to Thomas Telford's graceful suspension bridge of 1826, which carried all main road traffic for many years until the more prosaic bridge was built alongside, itself now replaced for through traffic by the Conwy Tunnel. The third bridge carries the main railway line from Crewe and Chester to Holyhead. The Telford bridge, with a restored tollhouse, is cared for by the National Trust.

Smallest house, Conwy

As would be expected in such a confined space, the town's shops are small, but with an interesting diversity. There is also a railway station with services on the North Wales main line. Close to the station is Conwy Visitor Centre.

Following the construction of the road tunnel in the 1980's, a 47 hectare nature reserve was formed on nearby land by the estuary, with islands and shallow lagoons, now host to an impressive array of waders, wildfowl and over 300 species of plants. Visitor centre, trails and hides are all wheelchair accessible.

The Walk

From the recommended car park take the pedestrian route under the railway, signposted to 'town centre'; bear left up steps or ramp to pass under the town wall. Turn right (Conwy Visitor Centre is a few metres to the left) to walk down to the square in front of the castle, with mini roundabout. Bear left to go under the wall to reach one end of the quay.

The three bridges are obvious to the right.

1. Turn left to walk along the quay, passing the 'smallest house'. Go under the wall yet again to reach a 'North Wales Path' signpost in 30 metres. Bear right here to follow an attractive surfaced path along the edge of the estuary, with Bodlondeb Wood on the left.

Conwy Estuary, Deganwy

The views across to Deganwy, the Great Orme and the mini peaks of the Vardre are very fine.

Just before reaching the far end of the wood turn left to follow a track rising through the trees; there is a waymark on a post. This leads to a little lane behind a school. Turn left along a residential road, Morfa Drive, soon crossing a main road.

2. Go over a railway footbridge, now following the North Wales Path, and rise steadily along a broad, gravelled, trackway. After passing the entrance to Beechwood Court, the track becomes tarmac surfaced. Bear right; the track loses its surface and the North Wales Path leaves on the right to continue its ascent of Conwy Mountain. We are still rising, now more gently.

3. 100m. or so before a prominent property turn left through an old kissing gate to a descent of a few rough steps and a narrow path. Cross a footbridge over a stream at the bottom, go through another kissing gate and rise diagonally left across a meadow; keep close to the left hand boundary to go to a kissing gate in the top corner.

To the right is good mountain scenery in the area of the Sychnant Pass.

Turn right along the roadside for less than 100 metres, then turn left through another of the by now very familiar kissing gates, signposted. After an initial short rise over grass, go over a ladder stile, pass a communications mast and go downhill to another kissing gate and an old path which threads its way between the gardens of modern housing. Join a residential road; continue to a more important road, turning left.

4. Join an even more important road in 50 metres turning left to walk along the roadside footpath back towards Conwy. At a road junction just outside the town wall bear right to take the pedestrian route under the wall.

Sculpture, Conwy Quay

There is an access point to the top of the wall here.

Turn right along Rosemary Lane and right again at the bottom to pass Conwy Visitor Centre. A further right turn retraces the pedestrian route under the wall, directly to the car park.

Walk 3: Sychnant Pass

A rare opportunity for 'level' walkers to enjoy true upland walking, with superb views in virtually all directions whilst circling around the top of Maen Esgob. Not a long walk but the total amount of rise and fall does demand a little more than usual effort, very worthwhile for those who can manage it.

Distance	4½ km (2¾ miles)
Ascent	Approximately 100m (328ft)
Underfoot	Generally very good, on pleasant grass paths. One section across a steep hillside is narrow, but without problems. No road walking. One ladder stile
Maps	Ordnance Survey Explorer OL17, Snowdon and the Conwy Valley, 1:25,000 Ordnance Survey Landranger 115, Snowdon, 1:50,000
Start/Parking	Small informal parking areas on either side of the road a short distance on the Penmaenmawr side of the top of the Sychnant Pass, the minor inland road connecting Conwy and Penmaenmawr. Grid reference 750770
Refreshments:	None en route

About the Area

The Sychnant Pass has long provided an inland alternative to the more obvious coastal route which was, before the construction of the modern tunnels, constrained by the great seaward thrust of the huge mound of Penmaenbach and was regarded by many travellers as hazardous. The narrow road over the Pass connects Conwy directly with Penmaenmawr and beyond. Nevertheless, it seems to be little

The Sychnant Pass

used by through traffic. It is not a high pass and the approach gradients on the Conwy side are hardly steep.

From the little car parking area immediately to the west of the summit the views of surrounding mountains, Altwen – 255m (837ft), Penmaen-bach – 10 metres lower and Mynydd y Dref (Conwy Mountain) – 11 metres lower, and over Dwygyfylchi and Penmaenmawr villages are superb. To the south of the Pass, the rather indeterminate mass of Maen Esgob reaches just over 300m (985ft).

The Walk

Right by the roadside is a 'North Wales Path' signpost. Follow the line indicated, over grass up towards a gate. Before the gate turn right along an inviting grass track with a 'walkers only' sign. The path climbs steadily, at a reasonable gradient. A dip in the ground is soon reached; the short rise on the far side is as steep as it gets.

The views to the sea over the village nestling below are superb.

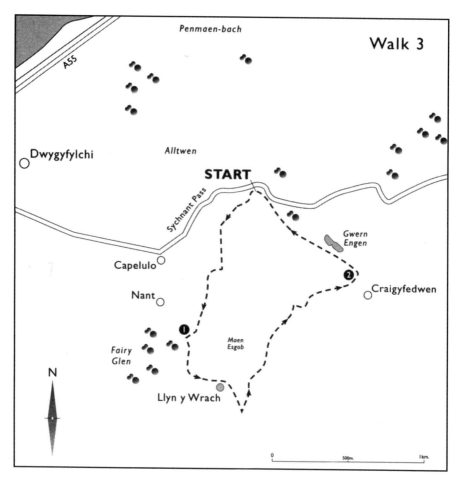

Continue around the head of a cwm above Capelulo on a narrow path across the heather clad hillside then bear left to head towards a prominent building, descending gently. Keep left at a minor fork to reach the corner of a farm wall.

1. Go forward for a few metres then turn left between walls to rise above the farm; the gradient soon eases. Keep close to the wall on the right for a short distance before bearing left on a good track along the bottom of a miniature valley, to a post waymarking the North Wales Path.

Go straight on, rising gently along a broad track, passing the tiny Llyn y Wrach.

Suddenly, there are views ahead, over the Conwy Valley.

The path bears to the left, towards a wall. Turn further to the left, 40 metres before the wall and continue.

The unspectacular summit of Maen Esgob, with small rock outcrops and abundant gorse is a little way to the left of our route as we reach our maximum height of almost 280m (919ft), with Conwy Castle and Deganwy in view.

Start the long descent quite close to the wall on the right for some distance, ignoring the occasional fork and then keeping well to the left of a prominent rock knoll.

2. As the track bends to the left at the bottom, leave it to turn left along a grass path aiming for a small lake, Gwern Engen. This area has many grass paths; the correct route goes just to the left of the water before rising gently to a ladder stile over a wall. Continue, with a wall on the right, down into a small depression, pass a sheepfold, bear right at a marker post and return to the gate just above the car park.

Walk 4: Trefriw

A truly level walk across the wide bottom of the Conwy Valley, connecting two of the most significant towns/villages. Pleasant riverside footpath for much of the distance.

Distance	6¾ km (4¼ miles)
Ascent	Negligible
Underfoot	Very good indeed. Close cropped grass and some tarmac. One potentially muddy section. Thirteen stiles
Maps	Ordnance Survey Explorer OL17, Snowdon and the Conwy Valley, 1:25,000 Ordnance Survey Landranger 115, Snowdon, 1:50,000
Start/Parking	Free car parking area just off the main B5106 in Trefriw, turn opposite Trefriw Woollen Mill. Grid reference 781630
Refreshments:	Good choice at each end of the walk

About the Area

Llanwrst is the principal settlement of the mid Conwy Valley, a business-like but not unattractive little town served by the Conwy Valley railway line connecting Llandudno Junction with Blaenau Ffestiniog and by the A470 main road. There are some good stone buildings and a range of shops, cafes and restaurants.

Probably the best known feature is the graceful old three arched bridge across the river, Pont Fawr, with an attractive old building, now a tea shop, adjacent.

Trefriw is more of an elongated village on the west side of the valley, set tightly at the foot of the steep, wooded, hillside, a northern extension of the Forest Enterprise Gwydyr Forest. Visitor attractions include the famous Trefriw Woollen Mill, open to visitors, at least in

The old bridge, Llanrwst

part, throughout the year and Trefriw Wells Spa, 2 km to the north, claimed to be of Roman origin, also open daily. Shops are sparse, but refreshments are available in the village.

The Walk

Walk back from the parking area towards the woollen mill, turning right along a signposted path passing tightly between public conveniences and the Afon Crafnant. The riverside footpath is initially between wire fences. Go over a stile and along a short unsurfaced roadway. Continue through an old kissing gate and along a grass path on the top of a raised embankment, a pleasant route keeping to the side of the Afon Crafnant for some distance. Pass a footbridge; do not cross but continue over a stile to reach the confluence of the Crafnant and Conwy rivers.

1. Bear to the right to walk beside the Afon Conwy, broad and placid in marked contrast to its character above Bettws-y-Coed. Go over a stile as the embankment becomes higher, presumably to improve its anti-flooding capacity. Go over another stile and pass 3 old oak trees. There are 2 more stiles then a tiny pond, followed by a larger pond, tucked away among trees.

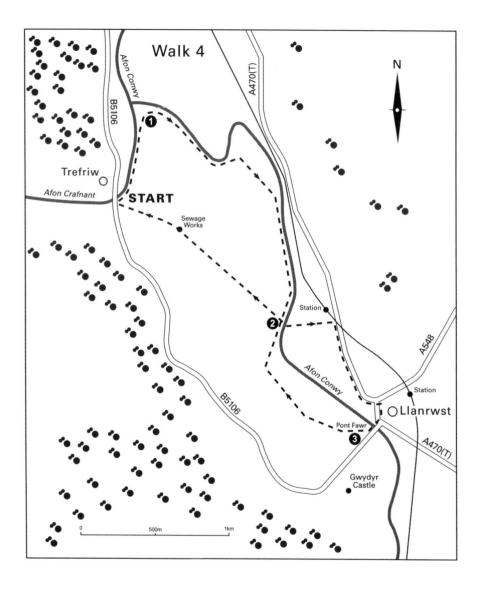

The Conwy Valley railway line is close across the water as the suspension bridge comes into view ahead, whilst to the right the Grey Mare's Tail waterfall can be seen among the woodland high on the valley side.

Go over a stile to reach a surfaced track, with a road to the right and the footbridge to the left.

2. Turn left over the footbridge to head into the northern part of Llanwrst. Pass a veterinary surgery to reach a more important road; Llanwrst North railway station is across the road to the left. Turn right, along the roadside pavement, soon reaching the A470; bear right to pass a car parking area with public conveniences.

   In the town centre go round to the right, still following the A470, to reach the Pont Fawr. Turn right, over the bridge, signposted 'Trefriw, B5106', passing the fine little tea room and gift shop building.

3. Turn right a few metres after the building at a public footpath signpost to take a broad track past a children's play area. As this lane bends to the left, go over a ladder stile and along the edge of a cultivated field, rare in this area. Go over a stile and along the edge of the next field, then over another stile to continue across this patchwork of small fields.

   The path is not always distinct on the ground, but the route is obvious enough. Go over another stile, cross a stream, over another stile and up the side of an embankment to a stile on the right in 10 metres. Go over and walk along the embankment towards the end of the suspension bridge. On reaching the roadway by the bridge, go over a stile and turn left across a concrete bridge to stroll back to Trefriw along this traffic free and very straight roadway leading directly to the car parking area. Towards the Trefriw end there is a path behind trees on the right which some walkers might prefer to use.

Walk 5: Llyn Crafnant

A fine short walk around a lake which sits in a cwm amongst the hills, with enough woodland (Forest Enterprises) to provide diversity in the landscape.

Distance	5 km (3 miles)
Ascent	60m (198ft)
Underfoot	Splendid – a forest roadway and a minor cul de sac public road. One very short section of rough track on the ascent/descent near Hendre. One ladder stile
Maps	Ordnance Survey Explorer OL17, Snowdon and the Conwy Valley, 1:25,000 Ordnance Survey Landranger 15, Snowdon, 1:50,000
Start/Parking	Pay and display car park with public conveniences, picnic tables and information board among the trees by the approach road to the lake. Leave the B5106 in Trefriw. Grid reference 756618. **Note:** For those who would like to avoid 200m or so up and down the road from the car park to the lake, there are a few roadside spaces by the end of the lake and there is also car parking (pay) at Cynllwydd, a little more than 1km further along the road
Refreshments:	Cafe and tea gardens at Cynllwydd

About the Area
The attractive valley containing Llyn Crafnant is very much at the end of the little road which climbs gently into the hills above Trefriw. From

Llyn Crafnant and the Richard James memorial

the head of the valley the only ways out are by footpaths over the hills to Llyn Geirionydd or Capel Curig. Between the rough hillside and the boggy valley bottom there is little enough fertile ground and the scant farming is restricted to sheep. The forested areas are off-shoots of the extensive Forest Enterprises Gwydyr Forest.

The lake itself, 1¼ km (¾ mile) long, is actually a reservoir but this is hardly apparent as there are no unsightly draw down lines at the shore. With some adjacent land, it was gifted in late Victorian times to the people of Llanwrst by Richard James as a public water supply. The grateful recipients erected the prominent memorial in 1896.

The Walk

From the main car park start along a little path angling up to the road, accompanied by the rushing rapids of Afon Crafnant, reaching the lake in 200 metres. Turn right by the memorial to pass the lower end

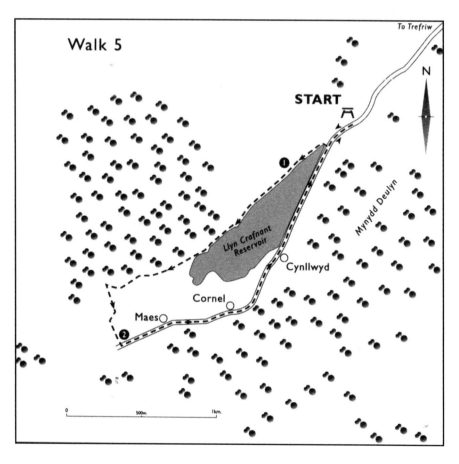

of the lake and follow a broad, easy, forest roadway. This track rises and falls just a little as it passes through light woodland, never far from the lake shore.

1. At a junction keep left by the lake side, passing a yellow capped post, one of many which officially mark this route. Pass the head of the lake, with the mountainous valley head now more dominant.

   The prominent peak is Craig Wen.

   After a marker post the track becomes narrower and rougher, rising for some distance.

Close to the top of the rise there are markers by a left turn down a steep and rather awkward little path. Turn here and go over a ladder stile to descend through young conifers, cross a bridge and join an access roadway below the houses, Hendre and Hendre Bach.

Turn left to continue downhill along the roadway, going straight on at a junction and passing two wooden bungalows before bearing round to the left.

2. Join a surfaced road at a field gate. Pass Maes Mawr Farm and then Cormel, nestling below the road, soon reaching the beautifully situated cafe/tea gardens, fishing and boating centre at Cynllwydd. No route finding is necessary on this return amble, just carry on to the monument and the car park.

Walk 6: Llyn Geirionydd

A pleasant stroll around a fine little lake in an attractive setting.

Distance	3 km (2 miles)
Ascent	Not more than 15m (49ft) in total
Underfoot	Surfaced road on one side of lake, footpath along tree-lined shore on the other side. The path has rather rough sections, with protruding tree roots. Incongruously for such a gentle walk, there is a tiny little scramble up and over a rib of rock. Three stiles
Maps	Ordnance Survey Explorer OL17, Snowdon and the Conwy Valley, 1:25,000 Ordnance Survey Landranger 115, Snowdon, 1:50,000
Start/Parking	Pay and display car park, with picnic tables, public conveniences and information boards. Accessed from Trefriw by minor roads climbing through Gwydyr Forest. Grid reference 764604
Refreshments	Bring your own picnic

About the Area
Llyn Geirionydd is an attractive lake 1¼ km (¾ mile) long, fringed by an open hillside on its eastern side and by woodland (an extension of the Forest Enterprises Gwydyr Forest) on its western side. The forested hill of Mynydd Deulyn rises to a maximum height of just over 400m (1313ft).

The car park occupies an area formerly covered by the waste tips of the New Pandora Mine from which lead ore was transported by tramway along the shore of the lake and by an aerial rope way to the

Klondike mill and mine, which was situated below the lake, in a part of the valley which had a great deal of industrial activity, both mining and quarrying. During the 20th century this became a derelict industrial landscape, now largely disappeared under the planting started by the then Forestry Commission in 1929.

There is a monument to the 6th century poet, Taliesin, at the northern end of the lake.

The Walk

Turn left to follow the public road.

1. Turn right in less than 200 metres, pass a vehicular barrier and walk along an access roadway past the head of the lake. Cross the main feeder stream. In 150 metres, as the main track rises sharply, turn right at a field gate/stile to take a pleasant grass path.

   Go over another stile to continue along a well marked path between trees, always close to the edge of the lake. There is some mud and

Llyn Geirionydd

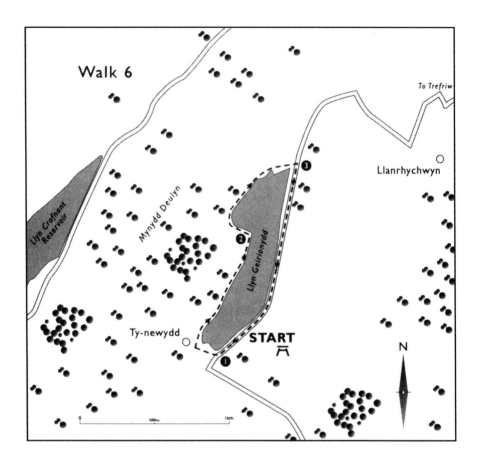

care is needed in negotiating the tree roots. Having said that, this is a delightful route along the rock strewn shore.

2. Towards the north end of the lake a little rocky spur descends from the main hill slope to the edge of the water. There is no alternative to scrambling over this unexpected obstacle, best done by following the marks left by others. Descend the rough path on the far side with care to reach a tiny stony beach.

The view ahead shows the visual advantage of diversification in planting trees, as on the left of the lake, compared with the boring conifer plantation on the right.

Cross a fence on a ladder stile to reach the foot of the lake, bearing right to follow waymarks on posts.

Above, to the left, is the monument.

Pass a small stone building, still bearing right, cross a dam at the foot of the lake and reach the public road at a kissing gate.

3. Turn right to walk along the grass beside this very quiet gated road to the car park.

Walk 7: Gwydyr Forest

A well varied circuit, largely in woodland, with industrial archaeology interest but which does have more rise and fall than most of the walks in the book. One suggestion is that 50m (155ft) of ascent along the road at the end of the walk could be obviated by stopping at the Hafna Mine and sending the fittest member of the party up the road to bring the car.

Distance	6 km (3¾ miles)
Ascent	155m (509ft)
Underfoot	Predominantly very good; forest roadways, footpaths and 1km. (²/₃ mile) of minor road. Some mud in wet weather. Four stiles
Maps	Ordnance Survey Explorer OL17, Snowdon and the Conwy Valley, 1:25,000 Ordnance Survey Landranger 115, Snowdon, 1:50,000
Start/Parking	Free roadside car park just past the Outdoor Education Centre. Leave the B5106 at Trefriw and follow the remarkable little road which climbs steeply to the south. There are alternative approaches from Llanwrst and Bettws-y-Coed. Grid reference 777591
Refreshments:	None

About the Area

Gwydyr Forest Park covers a large area of predominantly derelict industrial landscape, where extensive mining from the 1870's to about the time of World War I has left numerous shafts, adits and spoil

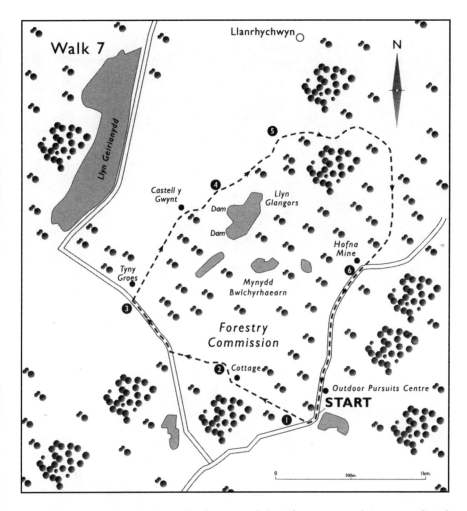

heaps. Most are now well disguised by forestry. This is upland country, attractive to walk, with the forest roadways contributing in providing good routes.

The Walk

From the car park turn left to walk along the little road, away from the Outdoor Centre, passing a largely silted small lake. On reaching a junction with a forest roadway, turn right at the wide, gated, entrance.

Remains of the Hafna Mine in Gwydyr Forest

1. Turn left at a junction in 100 metres along another broad forest roadway, with waymark. There are now yellow capped posts marking the way, as the track rises to pass a neat stone and slate cottage.

2. In 60 metres, after the cottage, fork left along a good footpath, still marked by the posts. Pass a protected old mine shaft, the first of many, and go straight across another forest road to continue along a grass path, steadily downhill. Cross a little stream and an area of rough ground, potentially wet. There is another muddy section before a public road is reached. Turn right to follow the road downhill for about 250 metres.

The splendid mountain skyline ahead includes the shapely Moel Siabod.

3. Turn right at a signposted access roadway to the detached house, Tyn y Groes. Pass to the right of the house, below heaps of mining spoil, to a field gate and a clear track rising across a meadow in this more open section of the walk. Pass the remains of an old mine, bearing to the right to rise gently to Castel y Gwynt Farm, with fine views to the mountains on the left, with the forest on the right. Go over a stile to cross the front of the farmhouse and exit by a similar stile to follow a grass path rising to the left.

Below, to the right, is Llyn Glangors.

4. A few metres after the next field boundary, with gate, bear to the right, towards the forest fence, and then go left along a rudimentary grass path. Go over a waymarked stile in about 200 metres. to enter the forest. A narrow but adequate path stays close to the edge of the forest before another stile is reached. Go over to leave the forest for a short distance, along a path just outside the boundary.

5. Go over a stile (waymark on far side) to re-enter the forest, cross a little stream and walk up to a forest roadway, broad and firm surfaced. Turn left to follow the roadway uphill at a gentle gradient.

Trefriw is visible, below left, through the trees.

Go straight on at a junction, now with views of the east side of the Conwy Valley. Go straight on at another junction, with more mine remains apparent along the way. The track now goes downhill for a considerable distance to join the public road beside the substantial remains of the Hafna Mine, of the late 19th century where lead and zinc ore were mined and there was also a smelter.

There is an interpretation board to the left of the track.

6. Pass the vehicular barrier to turn right and finish with an uphill roadside walk of a little more than 1km (¾ mile), passing a cottage, and a former chapel, now part of the outdoor education centre.

Dwellings, Gwydyr Forest

Walk 8: Betws-y-Coed

This 'double' walk makes good use of the limited amount of level ground around Bettws-y-Coed, firstly with a circuit largely around the golf course, bounded by the Afon Conwy and its tributary the Afon Llugwy, secondly by an out and back excursion to the well known Miners' Bridge, all in attractive surroundings.

Distance	5¾ km (3½ miles) in total
Ascent	Very little, less than 20m (66ft) in total
Underfoot	Part one, by the rivers and the golf course, is entirely first rate. The Miners' Bridge part has sections where tree roots and large stones combine to make a little care necessary. Four stiles
Maps	Ordnance Explorer OL17, Snowdon and the Conwy Valley, 1:25,000 Ordnance Survey Landranger 115, Snowdon, 1:50,000
Start/Parking	Extensive pay and display car park in Bettws-y-Coed, by the railway station. Grid reference 795566
Refreshments	A selection in Bettws-y-Coed

About the Area

The large village of Betws-y-Coed is one of the great visitor centres of North Wales, strategically situated where the steep sided valleys of the Conwy and the Llugwy rivers come together before continuing to Conwy and the sea as a wider, altogether more gentle, valley. For obvious reasons, this makes Bettws an important communications centre. The long branch railway line from Llandudno Junction to Blaenau Ffestiniog serves Bettws, and the A5 trunk road from London and the Midlands to Holyhead is the village main street. Happily, most

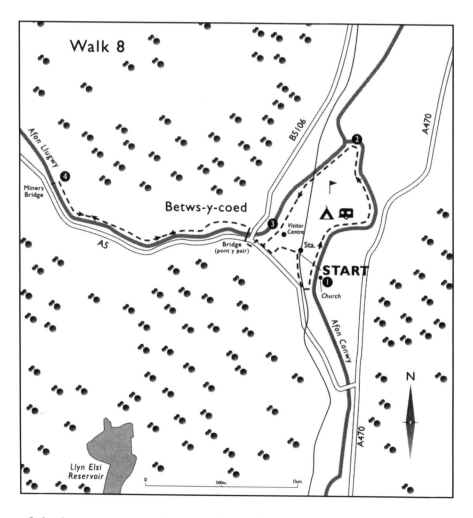

of the heavy transport is now diverted via the A55 expressway along the coast.

One of the great attractions has long been the Swallow Falls, approximately 4km (2½ miles) further upstream on the Afon Llugwy, a simple extension of the Miners' Bridge walk for those who are prepared for steady ascent.

Other attractions include the 14th century church of St. Michael, a railway centre behind the station, a motor museum and the Waterloo Bridge.

The Walk

For the full walk, go back along the station car park access road to its junction with the main road, passing public conveniences en route. Turn left at the main road, then left again in 100m., along a minor road signposted to the golf club and the railway centre.

1. Go over a railway bridge and head for a church.

   The railway centre is to the left. A small diversion to the right reveals a charming little suspension bridge over the river.

   At the church lych gate turn right then left at once, over an easy stile to pass along the edge of the churchyard. Exit by a similar stile to regain the tarmac roadway and pass between the Afon Conwy and a static caravan site. Pass a waymark on a post to take an excellent riverside path, by the entrance to the golf club, soon entering the course itself at an old kissing gate, duly noting the warnings.

   The route stays close to the river, always easy to follow and with all round views to the wooded hills above Bettws.

2. Leave the course briefly by a kissing gate at the far end and bear left to a seat strategically placed by the confluence of the Conwy and the Llugwy rivers. Continue round to the left to re-enter the golf course at a kissing gate and stay close to the pleasantly tree-lined banks of the Afon Llugwy. Leave the course by the side of a field gate, stay by the river and then go under an angled railway bridge. Pass a well-screened sewage works and then Royal Oak Farm Cottage before reaching the Stables Visitor and Crafts Centre, which is very close to the car park.

3. To continue with the second part of the walk, to the Miners' Bridge, in front of the visitor centre bear right towards the main street, reached by the Royal Oak Hotel. At the main street, turn right along the roadside pavement. At the first road junction, turn right to cross an old bridge, Pont y Pair, then turn left immediately towards the public conveniences. In 50 metres turn left at a footpath sign to follow a broad, well used, track through the trees, close to the

Suspension bridge at Betws-y-Coed

River Llugwy, most attractive hereabouts as it rushes between boulders in a series of rapids. There are rough sections of path but the way to the Bridge is never in doubt, with the audible presence of the river adding to the overall charm. Go over a waterside ladder stile and continue along a more open section, with a small footbridge across a tributary stream.

Cross over the remains of an old wall, pass one of the several waymarks on this route and re-enter woodland. Go over another ladder stile, cross a possibly boggy patch of ground and then make a minor ascent by an old mine entrance before reaching the celebrated bridge.

4. Turn around to retrace the route to Bettws. A left turn opposite the Royal Oak Hotel leads directly to the station car park.

Walk 9: Capel Curig and Llyn Ogwen

Right among the great mountains of Snowdonia, a straightforward, easy, out and back walk, allowing time to admire the grandeur of the scenery on both sides of the Nant Ffrancon Pass at a cost of very little ascent. A rare opportunity for 'level' walkers.

Distance	Full return walk 13km (8 miles). Shorter version 4½ km (2¾ miles)
Ascent	120m (394ft) Very well spread at easy gradients
Underfoot	A very good 'Landrover' track for most of the way, but there are boggy areas, mostly not difficult to avoid. There are several ladder stiles, mostly with openable gates beside
Maps	Ordnance Survey Explorer OL17, Snowdon and the Conwy Valley, 1:25,000 Ordnance Survey Landranger 115, Snowdon, 1:50,000
Start/Parking	Free car park at Capel Curig, behind the village shop/cafe, just a few metres from the A5 main road. Grid reference 721582. For the short walk there is a car park by the side of the A5. Walk to the nearby farm to pay. Grid reference 685603
Refreshments	None along the route. Capel Curig or Idwal

About the Area

The Nant Ffrancon is a very easy road pass creeping between the Carneddau and Glyder groups of mountains at a comparatively low level. The focal point of the pass is Idwal, with its famous youth hostel, refreshments and public conveniences, whilst the highest

Llyn Ogwen, on the Ffrancon Pass

point is a little way east of Llyn Ogwen. The mountain scenery is on a grand scale with favourites such as Tryfan, looming over the main road and our track, and the ice scraped north cwms of the Glyders contrasting with the more rounded humps of the Carneddau to the north of the Pass.

Capel Curig is a well spaced settlement, with general store, cafe and outdoor equipment shop, in a strategic position at the junction of the A5 and A4086 roads. It has long been a rallying point for expeditions to the nearby mountains.

The Walk

Turn right from the car park, go over a cattle grid and head for the mountains along a surfaced track. There is an 'Ogwen' signpost.

The first peaks to claim the attention are Pen yr Oleu Wen and Carnedd Daffyd, two of the giants of the Carnedd group. Soon, the Snowdon group is visible to the left.

Rise, but not excessively, to go through a field gate opposite a small farm, Gelli, where the track loses its surface. Apart from a little mud, the surface is still good.

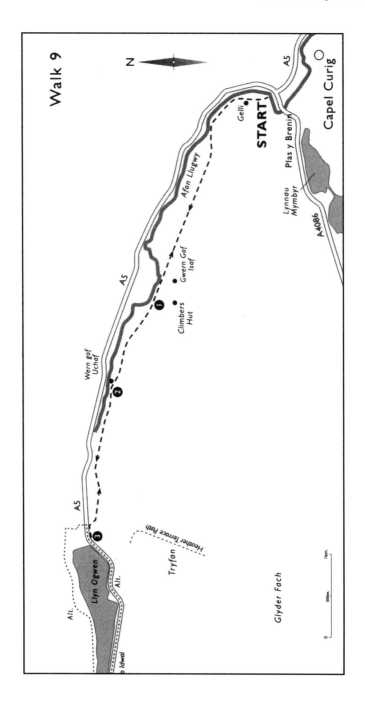

Walk 9

N

Capel Curig

A5

Gelli

START

Plas y Brenin

Lynnau Mymbyr

A4086

Afon Llugwy

A5

Gwern Gof Isaf

Climbers Hut

Wern gof Uchaf

Llyn Ogwen

Alt.

Alt.

Alt.

b Idwal

Heather Terrace Path

Tryfan

Glyder Fach

0   500m.   1km.

To the right the Afon Llugwy hustles along between gorse-lined banks in this increasingly sparsely vegetated landscape.

Bend to the left as a majestic mountain comes into view; this is Gallt yr Ogof, which might be mistaken for Tryfan on a gloomy day. Go through/over a field gate/ladder stile, the first of several on this route, and negotiate a boggy patch.

1. Enter National Trust land – Glyderau – below the cliffs of Gallt yr Ogof, with Tryfan soon coming into view in all its glory. Continue with a wall on the right and over a ladder stile, where a connecting path joins our route.

   Rise a little to approach a farm. Go through a gate, cross a stream on a bridge, pass the farm, Gwern Gof Isaf, with its camping field, cross the farm access drive and continue past a National Trust sign. To the left is a climbers' hut.

   (The short version of the walk joins the main route here). The summit of Glyder Fach can be seen.

2. Go over a ladder stile as the main road is approached and Llyn Ogwen comes into view. After another gate/ladder stile, pass above a small farm, Gwern Gof Uchaf, with Y Garn and Foel Goch now impressive ahead. Head for 'Tryfan' at a signpost. After more openable gates beside ladder stiles, bear right to join the main road. Turn left to walk to Llyn Ogwen along the roadside footpath.

3. At this point turn round to return to Capel Curig **or** continue by the roadside to Idwal **or** cross the road and follow the signposted footpath around the far side of the lake to Idwal (30m (98ft) extra ascent) and a little extra distance, but with better views. In either case, from Idwal return to Capel Curig by bus unless, of course, there is a kind friend providing a return by car.

   The shorter walk cuts across by Gwern Gof Uchaf to join the main route in a straightforward manner. From this starting place the return distance to and from Llyn Ogwen is about 4½ km (3 miles). The extension to and from Idwal would, of course add a little more to this modest distance.

Walk 10: Porthmadog and Tremadog

A well varied walk connecting the two main settlements of the Traeth Mawr. Some woodland, some waterside (Y Cyt - the cut), some Welsh Highland Railway and a little of the unlovely fringe of Portmadoc.

Distance	6½ km (4 miles)
Ascent	Negligible
Underfoot	Mixture of tracks and footpaths, all very good. Some surfaced road. Three stiles
Maps	Ordnance Survey Explorer OL18, Harlech, Porthmadog and Bala, 1:25,000 Ordnance Survey Landranger 124, Dolgellau, 1:50,000
Start/Parking	Several large car parks in Porthmadog. Park as close to the Harbour Station (or Tourist Information Centre) as possible. There is an extensive pay and display car park behind a large household store. If entering Porthmadog via the Cob, pass the Harbour Station and turn right immediately after crossing the river. Grid reference 570387
Refreshments	Inns and cafes at Porthmadog and Tremadog

About the Area

Until the early 19th. century the Glaslyn estuary, the large expanse of now mainly agricultural land known as Traeth Mawr was created by the efforts of William Madocks as part of his grandiose scheme to make tiny Porth Dinnlaen on the Lleyn Peninsula into the major port for the ferry traffic to Ireland. Madocks' main access road to the port would cross the estuary on a great embankment, with the final staging

post at the west end, a 'new town'
named Tremadog to be built by
Madocks.

Unfortunately for Madocks,
Holyhead became the ferry port
and the overall scheme failed.
However, despite immense
financial and technical problems,
he pushed on with the
embankment and the little town.
The Cob, as it has become known,
was finally completed in 1813,
subsequently providing a route for
the Ffestiniog Railway line and the
main road. The river diversion
through the Cob sluice gates was
soon instrumental in forming a
new natural harbour which,
coupled with the construction of

Signal box on the
Welsh Highland Railway

the railway line in 1836, was able to replace the previous not very
satisfactory arrangements as the principal outlet for the booming slate
industry of the Ffestiniog and other nearby valleys. So was formed the
port of Porthmadog, soon growing into a considerable town.

Today, Porthmadog has a good shopping centre and a range of
visitor facilities, with a fair amount of unappealing small
industry/commerce on the fringes. The visitor attractions include the
Ffestiniog and the Welsh Highland Railways and a Maritime Museum.

There is a railway station on the Cambrian Coast Line, with services
between Shrewsbury and Pwllheli.

In contrast, Madocks' new town of Tremadog has remained a quiet
place, with just a few shops, two inns and the unusual and attractive
Peniel Chapel.

Madocks himself lived at Tan-yr-allt on the Beddgelert road, whilst
T.E. Lawrence (of Arabia) was born at a house on the Porthmadog road
which is now a Christian mountain centre.

The Walk

Walk from the car park back towards the main street and the Tourist
Information Centre, close to the Ffestiniog Railway at Harbour

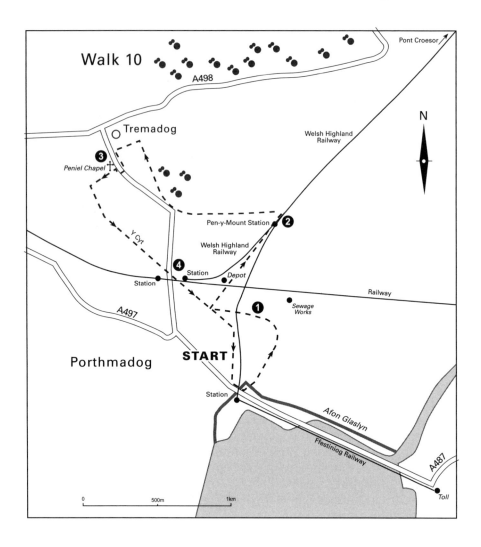

Station. Cross the road bridge over the river, heading for the Cob. In a few metres turn left into a broad roadway between properties. Pass a small worked out quarry and continue over a concrete bridge by the side of the sluices which control the flow of water to and from the former estuary. Carry on along a broad concrete path on a causeway, with water on each side.

1. Go left at a public road towards a large former mill, dated 1862. Pass the front of the mill and turn right, cross the railway line and continue along a roadway. In less than 100 metres turn right to cross The Cut on an old stone bridge and follow another roadway to the Cambrian Coast Railway Line.

   Go through a gate and cross the line, towards the depot of the Welsh Highland Railway. Follow the signs through the depot to reach a lineside footpath.

   The splendid mountain panorama around Traeth Mawr can now really be appreciated, Cnicht (the 'Welsh Matterhorn'), Moelwyn Fawr and Moelwyn Bach being particularly impressive. The railway depot has a good selection of the usual bits and pieces, including a neat little signal box.

   Continue by the side of the line, gorse now adding a blaze of colour, soon reaching the junction at Pen y Mount.

2. Go on to a gate with signpost. Turn left to cross the line and continue along a very quiet lane leading to the main road, A487, joined close to the entrance to Bodawen, a Madocks building now used as a nursing home. Cross the road and turn right to walk along the pavement for 150 metres, passing a most unusual feature, a modern stone circle constructed for the National Eisteddfod, held here in 1987.

   Re-cross the road to a signposted path into woodland. Go over a stepped stile and follow a broad track beside a drainage waterway. The pleasant deciduous wood is carpeted with primroses in spring. At the northern edge of the wood turn left along another wide track to return to the main road.

3. For the direct return to Porthmadog turn left to reach the Peniel Chapel in rather more than 100 metres. Turn right, over a stepped stone stile to take a footpath which leads to a kissing gate before joining the track which runs alongside The Cut. Turn left here.

   (To visit the middle of Tremadoc, turn right on joining the main road.)

After the left turn by The Cut, continue along the track by the waterway as far as the main road on the fringe of Porthmadog, reached at the Queens Hotel.

4. Cross the road and walk to the Welsh Highland railway station and tea room. Just before the station go over a stile on the right to cross the Cambrian Coast railway line and walk along an embankment with a footpath signpost. The Cut is still on the left. Reach a roadway, now approaching the large mill passed near the start of the walk. At the junction by the side of the mill, go straight across to a track which leads directly into the recommended car park. For any other car park continue to the main street close to the Tourist Information Centre.

Birth place of T.E. Lawrence, Tremadog

Walk 11: Portmeirion and Minffordd

This walk around the headland ('penrhyn') which separates Traeth Mawr and Traeth Bach has a relatively high proportion of rise and fall, passing close to the highest point on the headland. This is, however, a very pleasant area with wide ranging views from the selected route, making the necessary effort well worthwhile. It can be combined with a visit to the unique attraction of Portmeirion village.

Distance	4½ km (2¾ miles)
Ascent	135m (443ft)
Underfoot	Good tracks and surfaced roadways. Short distance along pavement by public road. Two stiles
Maps	Ordnance Survey Explorer OL18, Harlech, Porthmadog and Bala, 1:25,000 Ordnance Survey Landranger 124, Dolgellau, 1:50,000
Start/Parking	Roadside parking spaces 100 metres from the eastern end of the Cob. Grid reference 584379
Refreshments:	Minffordd. Portmeirion if visited

About the Area

The 'headland between two waters' is pleasant walking country, well provided with good, wide, tracks. Although the overall height is only a modest 81m (266ft), views across both estuaries are a fine feature. The gem of the headland is undoubtedly Portmeirion village, a remarkable place created from nothing by the vision and energy of one man, Clough Williams Ellis. Ellis selected a south facing sheltered site by the Traeth Bach, then from 1925 to 1972 Portmeirion grew, building by building, in an Italianate style, hotel, shops and other buildings all in perfect harmony with one another and with the

Ffestiniog locomotive at Minffordd

environment, which includes sandy beaches and sub tropical gardens. The village has been kept in private ownership and is operated as a visitor attraction, with its only public entrance from the large car parks at the north-eastern end. The distinctive Portmeirion pottery is world famous.

Minffordd, straggling along the A487 main road, is a much more workaday place. It does, however, have a few shops and two railway stations, one on the Cambrian Coast line and the other on the preserved Ffestiniog Railway.

The Walk

Cross the road and walk up a stony track with bridleway and footpath signs. Cross the line of the Ffestiniog Railway close to Boston Lodge Halt.

The famous railway works are a short distance to the right.

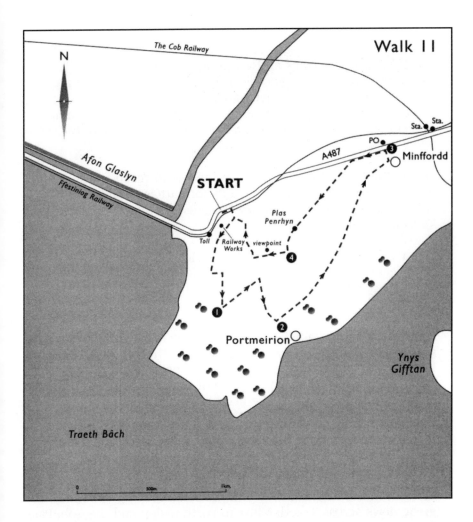

Go over a stile and continue uphill to a junction in less than 50 metres. Turn right to ascend along a fine track above and behind Boston Lodge Works. Go through a field gate as the gradient eases and the views across the estuary open up.

There is gorse by the wayside as the track kinks left then right to cross a meadow.

1. Turn sharp left at a sign to pass a farm.

Cnicht and the two Moelwyns are dominant ahead.

Join a farm access track and go straight on, passing a small pond
with a tiny island. Join another path immediately before a cattle
grid, turning right at another sign 'Port Meirion' to walk downhill,
through gateways in old walls. Go through a gate and continue the
descent as far as the Port Meirion restricted area, where there are
two barred gates.

2. Follow the footpath sign round to the left to reach a ladder stile;
   do not go over; turn right along a minor path leading to the village
   car parks. Away to the right is a tarmac road leading to the pay
   kiosk at the entrance.

   If not visiting the village, bear left to leave the main car park by
   the access road. At a cross roads just beyond the car park, go
   right, then left in 10 metres to a footpath signposted 'footpath to
   main road'.

   Follow this path, rising in parallel with the access road, soon with
   good views to the right over Traeth Bach to the hill country behind
   Harlech. Pass a tennis court and nursery gardens on the right and
   rejoin the tarmac road. On one side of the road or the other there
   are good footpaths, with the occasional signpost, all the way to
   Minffordd. Join a more important road, turning left for a short
   distance.

3. Turn left at the main A487, close to the post office in Minffordd,
   to walk uphill on the roadside pavement for 200 metres. Turn left
   at a very minor surfaced road and rise steadily along this road, with
   great views across Traeth Mawr to Porthmadog and the Cob. Pass
   Plas Penrhyn, home of the late Bertrand Russell, then a largely
   ruinous farm with a cattle grid, to reach a meeting place of tracks
   with a three way signpost, just before a pond.

4. Fork right, up a rise. In 20 metres fork right again, along a grass
   track, still rising. In a short distance look out for a tall, slim,
   standing stone to the right, marking the highest point of the
   headland and worth a short diversion for the wonderful breadth
   of the views.

Back to the path, continue downhill; at a fork keep left, close to an old stone wall, soon reaching a gate, a few steps and a major track. Turn right, downhill, to return to the car parking area, going through three gates, rejoining the outward route and crossing the railway line on the way.

Walk 12: Penrhyndeudraeth and the slate wharves

This is a very scenic and well varied route, a circuit to which an out and back section of about 1¾ km (1¼ miles) has been added. Apart from the industrial history, it includes the Ffestiniog Railway and an area of salt marsh noted for its population of waders and other birds.

Distance	7½ km (4¾ miles)
Ascent	100m (328ft), the majority at the start of the walk. No steep gradients
Underfoot	No difficulties. One ladder stile
Maps	Ordnance Survey Explrorer OL18, Harlech, Porthmadog and Bala, 1:25,000 Ordnance Survey Landranger 124, Dolgellau, 1:50,000
Start/Parking	Car park with public conveniences 200 metres or so along A 4085 from the main cross roads in the village. Grid reference 611391
Refreshments:	Inns and cafes at Penrhyndeudraeth

About the Area

The countryside between Penrhyndeudraeth and the Afon Glaslyn is an attractive mixture, fairly gently up and down and with woodland. The focal point of this walk is Tyddyn Isa, one of the six substantial slate wharves built along the riverside to allow the transfer of slate from the Blaenau Ffestiniog area from pack animals and carts into boats. In the 19th century slate was the absolutely dominant force of the local economy and the construction of the Tyddyn Isa wharf in

Slate wharf at Tyddyn Isa, near Penrhyndeudraeth

1825 was an important step forward in the difficult business of moving large quantities of slate from the comparatively remote quarries to users throughout the country.

The wharves remained in use for most of the century, also being used for importing gunpowder needed for the quarries; the two small buildings remaining at the site were gunpowder stores.

Penrhyndeudraeth is a not unattractive small town with inns, cafes, banks and shops, predominantly on flat land at the foot of a hillside. The A487 traverses the town and there are widely separated railway stations on the Cambrian Coast line and on the Ffestiniog Railway.

The Walk

Leave the car park and turn right along B4085, at first quite steeply uphill. The gradient soon eases; follow the road past the Ffestiniog railway station, then go over the line at the level crossing.

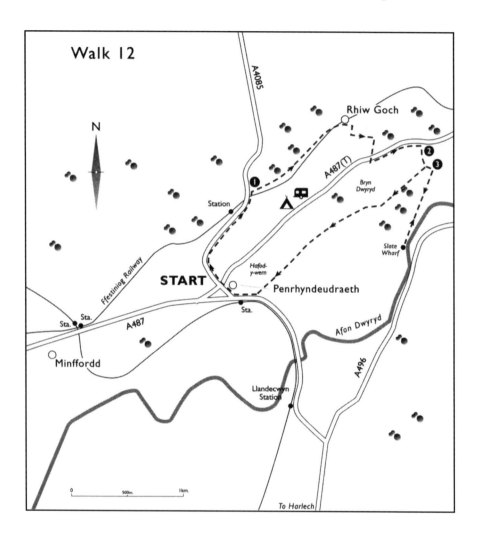

1. In 40 metres turn right into a surfaced lane. Follow this lane, rising a little and generally close to the railway line, heading towards Rhiw Goch, initially with a belt of conifers fringed with gorse to the left, reaching more open country after a field gate.

   There are splendid views of the Moelwyns and of the old buildings of Rhiw Goch ahead.

On reaching the buildings turn right, as indicated by a bridleway sign, go over a cattle grid and descend on a good track through a field gate, and across the railway line, with gates on each side, to farm buildings.

Turn sharp left immediately before the buildings, go through a gate and keep a wall close on the left hand as the ill defined path on grass heads for a gate giving access to coniferous woodland. In the wood the path is much clearer, descending gently to the main A487, reached at a field gate. Go through the gate, turn left and follow the roadside for 400 metres.

2. After passing a detached cottage on the left, turn right at a 'footpath' sign in 40 metres. Go down a few steps and over a ladder stile beside a stream, soon turning right to a field gate, a tiny stream and a rise, to join a very minor surfaced road at another gate.

(A right turn here produces a shortened route, omitting the slate wharf.)

To continue to the wharf turn left, then bear right in 50 metres at a footpath sign.

There is a small board with information about the marshes and the ducks, curlews, herons and other birds which can be seen by the wayside at different times of the year.

3. Proceed through a wooden gate and then through two field gates by old agricultural buildings. The delightful path has, significantly, broken slate underfoot, with deciduous woodland to the right and the riverside marshes to the left. Go through a kissing gate and along a corridor between the gorse.

The end of the trail is at the wharf, where two old buildings and about 200 metres of quay consisting of huge stone blocks remain, together with stone mooring bollards.

Beyond the wharf a tiny sand beach is on private land, not accessible to the public.

4. Set off back to the junction, reached just beyond point 3. and stay with the surfaced lane, passing a field gate before reaching Bryn Dwyryd Farm. The lane makes a fine return route gently up and down, with the estuary soon coming into view. A final descent leads to the Harlech to Porthmadog road.

5. Turn right to walk along the roadside for about 250 metres. Opposite Penrhyndeudraeth railway station (Cambrian Coast line) turn right, cross the main A487 and continue along High Street back to the car park.

Walk 13: Pont Croesor and Pont Talyrni

A rare offering of an out and back (or pick up by a non-walking companion) route which provides an attractive and well varied walk, two thirds totally flat and the other third having a comparatively gentle rise along a surfaced lane. Wide open spaces, mountain views and lovely old woodland are all included.

Distance	4 km (2½ miles) one way
Ascent	35m (115 ft) one way. 65m (213 ft) out and back
Underfoot	In the first kilometre there are sections of cattle-churned land, some of it not too pleasant for walking, particularly during a spell of wet weather. Thereafter, the surfaces are first rate, close cropped grass and a very pleasant lane. Four stiles (one way)
Maps	Ordnance Survey Explorer OL18, Harlech, Portmadoc and Bala, 1:25,000 Ordnance Survey Landranger 124, Dolgellau, 1:50,000
Start/Parking	There are a few off road parking spaces on either side of Pont Croesor, grid reference 593414. If a non-walking driver is to pick up at the far end, there is a roadside layby 250 metres north of Pont Talyrni
Refreshments:	Take a picnic

Traeth Mawr

About the Area

Traeth Mawr is a huge expanse of agricultural land created by Madocks' scheme (see walk no. 10), flat apart from a few rocky former islands. This expanse is crossed by the trackbeds of the former narrow gauge Croesor Tramway and the Welsh Highland Railway. The former fed the slate from the quarries in the Croesor Valley to the harbour at Portmadoc, its line later being joined by the Welsh Highland following the extension of that railway in 1923 from Dinas Junction on its ambitious route through Snowdonia. The line was closed in 1937. Following comprehensive renovation by the Ffestiniog Railway, little trains steam again across the wide expanse of Traeth Mawr.

Much of the walk has wide views of the mountains, Cnicht and the two Moelwyns being particularly prominent.

The Walk

There is a signposted footpath close to the north eastern end of Pont Croesor, a long bridge over a wide part of the Afon Glaslyn, with a low

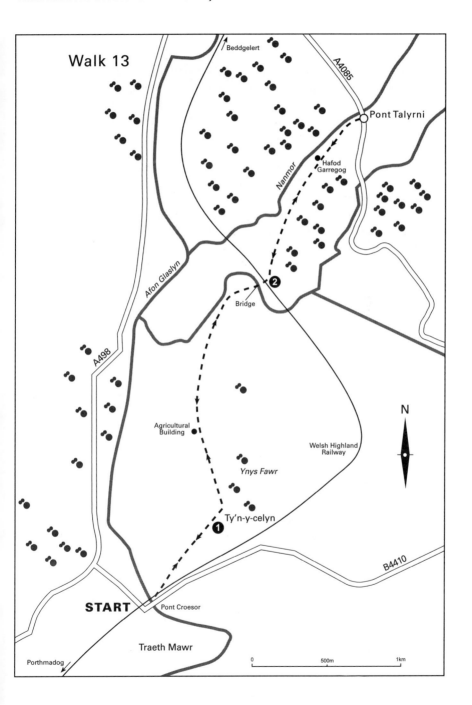

weir on the downstream side. On the upstream side, a new bridge has been constructed to carry the restored railway line. Cross the line by the two stiles and follow the indicated route across a reedy meadow, rather soft in places and not well defined on the ground. The line is towards the left hand end of the buildings of Ty'n-y-Celyn Farm, which sit cosily at the foot of what was obviously much the largest of the rocky islands of this former estuary.

Dominant in the mountain views is Cnicht, the 'Welsh Matterhorn'.

Go over a waymarked ladder stile and continue the same line across a huge meadow, reasonable underfoot until the final 100 metres or so before the farm, where there is a cattle-churned area. Cross a ditch on a footbridge and carry on to a waymarked stile immediately to the left of a large agricultural building.

1. Go over the stile in a stone wall and bear right, round the end of the building, to head for a waymarked gate in 60 metres. Turn sharp left after the gate to follow a wide track with a ditch and stone wall on the right. Continue along the top of a low embankment, then through a field gate to pass extensive gorse on the left and an outgrown hedge on the right and reach a double agricultural building. Follow the waymarks around the back of the building to go over a stile. The route stays with the low embankment, excellent underfoot, passing a plantation of mixed woodland to head for a substantial wooded rocky mound, which marked the head of the former estuary.

    The Snowdon mountain range is in clear view behind the mound.

    The embankment bends gently to the right, with a gate/stile and more gorse, soon approaching a footbridge. Leave the embankment to walk across to the bridge.

2. Go through a gate, left then right to bypass a tied up gate and continue the same line, now on a surfaced lane. The lane rises steadily for some distance, with wooded high ground to the right and the shallow wooded valley of the Afon Nanmoor on the left. Over the top of the rise, pass Hafod Garregog, an old dwelling, on the left and continue, joining the public road beside Pont Talyrni.

This is the turning point, unless you have a rendezvous at the roadside layby 250 metres to the left.

Walk 14: Morfa Harlech and Traeth Bach

The walk is across varied farmland to the north of Harlech, with some gentle ascent and wonderful views across the Traeth Bach estuary to Borth-y-Gest, Portmadoc and Portmeirion.

Distance	5 km (3 miles)
Ascent	50m (164 ft) in total
Underfoot	Very good tracks, lanes and short grass
Maps	Ordnance Survey Explorer OL18, Harlech, Portmadoc and Bala, 1:25,000 Ordnance Survey Landranger 124, Dolgellau, 1:50,000
Start/Parking	Several informal parking area at the northern edge of Morfa Harlech coniferous plantation. Turn west off the A496 main road along a minor surfaced roadway, signposted to a recycling centre, 2½ kilometres (1½ miles) north of Harlech railway station. Drive almost to the end of this road, but do not pass the recycling centre. Grid reference 583339
Refreshments:	Picnic only (some fine spots)

About the Area

Harlech is best known for its great castle, with Caernarfon and Conway forming a trio which King Edward I constructed along the coast of North Wales in the 13th century in order to subjugate the Welsh. The little town grew on the steep ground around the castle, formerly the shoreline. There are inns, cafes and shops.

Glan y Mor, north of Harlech

Over the centuries the sea has greatly receded from Harlech, producing the low-lying land at the start of this walk. The higher ground in the Ynys area to the north must have been an island.

The Walk

Walk away from the direction of the main road, towards the recycling centre. Shortly before reaching the centre, at the corner of the plantation, turn right, to a waymarked ladder stile. Go over and follow a path over grass, with the woodland on the right, to reach another ladder stile. Keep close to a wall; the landscape has now changed significantly, with higher ground ahead, a farmstead, and views to Moel-y-Gest across the estuary. Leave the wall to bear left across the meadow to a ladder stile and on to the farm of Glan-y-Mor, over yet another ladder stile.

1. Turn right, in front of the farm, along the farm access track. In 70 metres turn left at a waymarked gate, along another farm road; the estuarial views are superb. Go over/through a ladder stile/small gate in 100 metres and pass along the front of Gan-y-Morfa farmhouse, to head for a waymarked ladder stile. The route continues over grass, at the foot of a steep hillside, before bearing right on approaching a rocky topped knoll, beginning to rise gently to a waymark on a fence post and a ladder stile. Cross a tiny stream

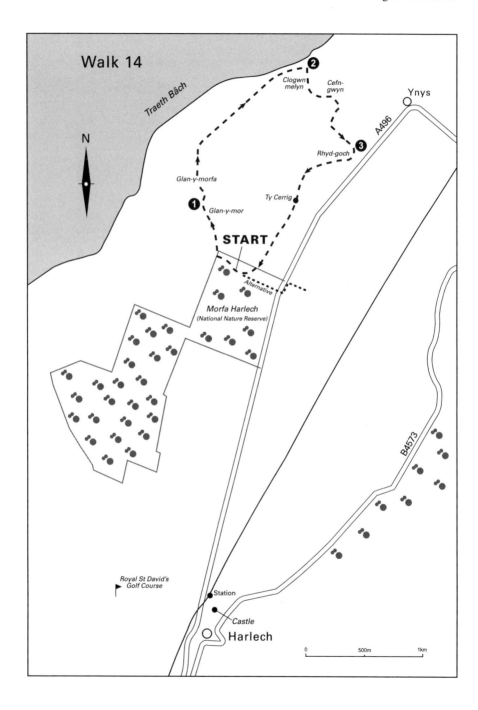

Walk 14

N

Traeth Bâch

Clogwn melyn

Cefn-gwyn

Ynys

A496

Rhyd-goch ❸

❷

Glan-y-morfa

Ty Cerrig

❶ Glan-y-mor

START

Alternative

Morfa Harlech
(National Nature Reserve)

B4573

Royal St David's
Golf Course

Station

Castle

Harlech

0   500m   1km

and aim for the lowest point at the top of this gradual rise. There are diffuse paths but all seem to go in the same general direction.

At the far end of this mini pass yet more views appear, particularly of Portmeirion, sitting prettily on its wooded hillside across Traeth Bach.

Go over a ladder stile and turn left to go slightly downhill, through a gap in a stone wall. Keep above the fence on the left and pass between great clumps of gorse to reach a house, Clogwyn Melyn.

2. Turn right to follow the access road, steadily uphill to a farm, Cefn-gwyn. Pass through and descend along a charming lane, with banks of primroses and wild violet under the thorn blossom in spring.

3.. In less than half a mile, just before a dwelling, look out for a signposted ladder stile on the right. Go over and follow the indicated line across a rough field. Bear right at a waymarked post at the far boundary. Turn left at a waymarked stile; a faint track now heads for Ty Cerrig Farm. Go through the farm then, as the road bends to the left, go straight across a meadow to cross another roadway to a waymarked kissing gate. Go through and continue across a large meadow to a waymarked fence post. Bear slightly right, keeping the fence and gorse on the left to head for the plantation. Go over a ladder stile, then another, to enter the woodland. At a junction of paths in 50 metres turn right, soon reaching the access road leading directly to the car park.

Walk 15: Criccieth and Llanystumdwy

An interesting circuit with fine views, connecting the holiday town of Criccieth with the village of Llanystumdwy, famous as the birthplace and home of David Lloyd George, one of the great prime ministers of the 20ᵗʰ century. Included is a length of the coastal path.

Distance	7 km (4½ miles)
Ascent	75m (246ft), the great majority on the return minor road
Underfoot	Good paths, minor road and surfaced lanes, with a short section along stony beaches. No really steep gradients
Maps	Ordnance Survey Explorer 13, Lleyn Peninsula East, 1:25,000 Ordnance Survey Landranger 123, Lleyn Peninsula, 1:50,000
Start/Parking	Small car park near to western extremity of Marine Terrace, Criccieth. Grid reference 495377. Also a fair amount of street parking along Marine Terrace
Refreshments:	Inn and cafe at Llanystumdwy. Abundant choice at Criccieth

About the Area

Sitting below and around the ruins of the castle on its rocky promontory, Criccieth is a neat little seaside town with a sandy beach and other attractions, such as pitch and putt golf, tennis and bowls, for holidaymakers. As would be expected, there are also plenty of shops, inns and cafes. Criccieth has a station on the coastal railway line, with services to Pwllheli, Portmadoc, Barmouth, Dolgelly and Shrewsbury.

The castle played an important part in the medieval conflict between the native Welsh and the invading English; constructed originally by the Welsh under Llewelyn the Great early in the 13th century, it was captured by the forces of King Edward I in 1283. It was then enlarged and reinforced and was able to withstand a long siege by the Welsh ten years later. Capture and burning by Owain Glyn Dwr in 1404 marked the end of the castle's period of useful life. Now owned and managed as a visitor attraction by Welsh Heritage (CADW), the castle is noteworthy for the fine gatehouse, unique in a castle built by Llewelyn.

Lloyd George at Llanystumdwy

Llanystumdwy is a rather scattered village, a little way inland, noteworthy as the birthplace of David Lloyd George, whose long career as an outstanding statesman included a term as prime minister during the latter part of World War I and the ensuing years. His presence is still very much felt in the village, with the Lloyd George Memorial Museum, the burial place and two houses which he occupied at different times. All are on the line of this walk.

The Walk

Walk towards the sea and turn right to go through a signposted modern gate and along a path initially by the side of a fence, keeping close to the sea. The access drive to Cefn Castell is soon reached. Go to the right, round the back of the house, then turn left immediately to resume close to the sea.

The views are extensive, including distant parts of the Lleyn Peninsula, with the Rivals (Eir Eifel) mountains and Garn Bentyrch.

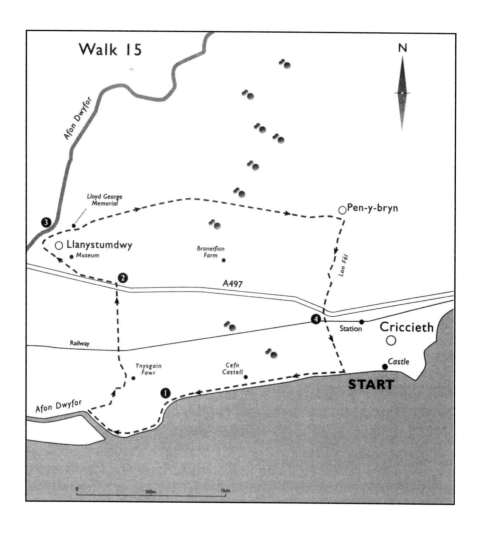

Pass the Ynys Gain National Trust sign and continue along the back of the beach for a few metres before reverting to a path on the right. Pass a track on the right then, at a junction, another track bends towards Ynysgain Farm.

1. Keep left here. Gorse is the dominant vegetation as we bear left towards a minor low headland, with a substantial reed bed on the right. The path is again pushed to the back of the beach, this time

by impenetrable gorse. Carry on to the mouth of the Afon Dwyfor, bearing right to follow the bank as far as two corrugated iron sheds, passing a ruined boat and plenty of shoreline debris at this former tiny harbour. Turn sharp right by the sheds and proceed along a lane. Go through/over a gate/stile and continue to another gate/stile and a junction with the roadway serving Ynysgain Fawr. Bear left to rise to a bridge over the railway line and reach the main road, A497.

2. Turn left to walk along the roadside pavement for about 200 metres, then fork right into Llanystumdwy village.

   The Lloyd George Museum and the public conveniences are well signposted.

3. Pass through the village to the bridge over the Afon Dwyfor; do not cross, but turn right to rise along a minor road, passing a long terrace of solidly built stone cottages.

   In a short distance, on the left, is Lloyd George's grave and a discreet monument.

   Pass a very old stone house as the road continues to rise; occasional wooded sections, with rhododendrons, add to the variety of the scenery as progress is made and there are some glimpses of the sea.

   The mountains visible to the left include Moel Hebog.

   Pass the lodge to Broneifion Farm, followed by another slight rise. Criccieth Castle comes into view; as the residential estate at Pen-y-Bryn is approached, turn right at a road junction to begin the descent to Criccieth along Lon Fel, a delightful surfaced lane; note the walls built of massive stone blocks, some being ancient field boundaries with earth bankings, as in the West Country. Cross the main road.

4. Follow a minor road signposted to the beach and the castle. Cross the railway line on a bridge and descend to the car park.

Walk 16: Beddgelert

An interesting but quite demanding short walk with the necessary effort well repaid by the proximity of the mountains, the fine village and the views generally.

Distance	5¾ km (3½ miles)
Ascent	130m (427ft) in total. More than half of this total occurs on the outward path of the route and is gradual. The rise to Perthi is steeper
Underfoot	Very good for the great majority of the route. The descent from Perthi to the A498 road has about 250 metres of awkward mountain-type track, descending quite steeply, with rocks and encroaching undergrowth. Three stiles
Maps	Ordnance Survey Explorer OL17, Snowdon and the Conway Valley, 1:25,000 Ordnance Survey Landranger 115, Snowdon, 1:50,000
Start/Parking	Pay and display car park in Beddgelert, accessed from A498, close to the Royal Goat Hotel. Grid reference 588482
Refreshments	To suit all tastes in Beddgelert

About the Area

Beddgelert is one of the finest old villages in Snowdonia, as near to being pretty as any settlement in this hard mountain landscape. The confluence of Afon Glaslyn and Afon Colwyn is right in the middle and there are attractive buildings, because of the geography more clustered than is normal in the area. Shops, inns and cafes provide for the considerable numbers of visitors; in high season Beddgelert is a very busy place indeed.

Snowdon itself is quite close by; the Snowdon Ranger and Watkin paths are popular routes to the summit but not, of course, for 'level' walkers!

From the early 1920's until 1937 the Welsh Highland Railway passed through Beddgelert. From 2009 the hard puffing and the shriek of locomotive whistles has again become a feature of village life, with the station a focal point for many visitors.

The legend of Gelert concerns the faithful hound of Llewelyn, the last 'real' Prince of Wales. The hound's grave is not far from the village centre, easily reached by the diversion set out below; the story is set out on a tablet beside the grave.

The Walk

Walk back from the car park to the A498 main road and turn right. In a few metres turn right, along a road rising beside the Royal Goat Hotel, ('bridleway' signpost), passing a modern residential development.

1. Turn right, along a stony track just above the hotel. In a short distance go through a gate on the right to pass below Beddgelert station; the views of mountains and village are superb. Go through a gate and pass under the railway. Cross a stream and reach another gate, giving access to a lane. Turn left to rise along the lane, with a stream gurgling on the left. Cross the railway line, pass a farm and reach a belt of woodland. Cross the railway yet again before reaching another farm.

2. Immediately beyond the buildings turn right, through a gate with bridleway waymark. Follow a clear track across the hillside. At a waymarked post fork right to stay with the bridleway, through a gate, and along a grass track; there is a wall close on the left for a considerable distance. There are more waymarked gates and a stream to cross before a forest roadway is reached. Turn right, downhill. Pass a vehicular barrier before joining another forest roadway. Turn left, with the railway now on the right and a caravan/camping site beyond. Pass a tiny railway platform.

3. At a junction of roadways bear right to cross the railway and

Beddgelert

descend gently along a surfaced road through the caravan site. Pass the reception and other buildings before rising gently to the main road, crossing the Afon Colwyn.

4. Turn right, downhill, along the roadside for approximately 200 metres then turn left, through a metal gate, into a grass lane between walls. Go up the lane for 40 metres then turn right, at a 'footpath' sign on a post, by the end of a stone wall, to walk over cropped grass, with a broken wall on the right. Cross a house access drive and rise rather steeply up a trackway. The gradient soon eases. Go through a gate and continue along the same excellent track, bear left over a brow, with bird's eye views over part of Beddgelert, passing a few old trees and a great deal of gorse. After a 'footpath' sign on a post, go round the back of the farmhouse on a cattle-churned track.

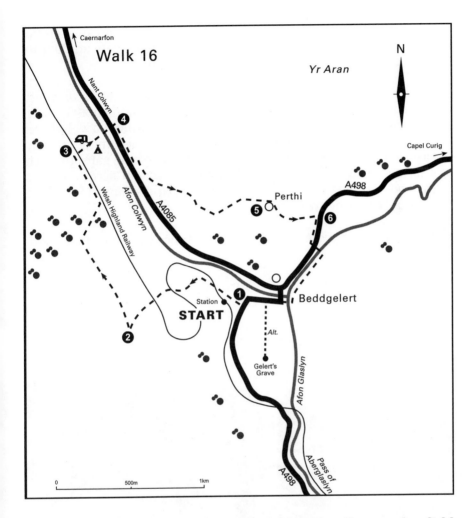

5. Descend through a gate and cross a field diagonally towards a field gate opening, with a plank bridge across a stream. Do not cross the stream but carry on down past a marker post on the right, to a metal gate. Go through and continue, with the wall and stream on the left, heading for a little gate in the bottom left corner, where there is a footpath sign. Bear left, with the wall close on the left for the awkward descent previously mentioned. The path is well worn, dividing in places where particular obstacles have been avoided but, in general, it stays close to the wall. Cross the stream amongst

rhododendrons before descending steeply to the back of a group of houses, passing a sign on a post. Go through a gate and out to the main road, where there is a 'footpath' sign.

6. Turn right, towards Beddgelert. In less than 200 metres turn left at a road junction and cross the Afon Glaslyn. Immediately after the bridge turn right, over a ladder stile, to follow a delightful riverside path, a little rough at first but soon becoming entirely easy, amongst rhododendrons. Go through two small gates to reach a tarmac road by the end of a bridge. Go straight across to pass the end of a long terrace of houses, then cross a footbridge at the confluence of the two rivers.

To visit Gelert's grave is a 400 metre diversion along a surfaced path after the bridge.

Otherwise, continue along a surfaced roadway to join the main road at the end of the village centre bridge. Keep straight on by the roadside before turning right to return to the car park.

Walk to Gelert's grave, Beddgelert

Walk 17: Tanygrisiau

A circuit of a sizeable reservoir, but not a gentle stroll by the edge of the water as might be expected. A fair amount of up and down and some pretty rough lengths of footpath make this a more demanding walk than its short length would indicate. Very rewarding for mountain views, the Ffestiniog Railway and industrial history.

Distance	4½ km (2¾ miles)
Ascent	90m (295 ft) in three main sections, including the odd steep little rise
Underfoot	Generally good with fine footpaths and some surfaced road but also sections of rough path. Nine stiles
Maps	Ordnance Survey Explorer OL18, Harlech, Porthmadog and Bala, 1:25,000 Ordnance Survey Landranger 124, Dolgellau, 1:50,000
Start/Parking	Large free car park on the road leading from the A496 to the Ffestiniog Power Station at Tanygrisiau. Grid reference 685449
Refreshments	Lakeside Cafe at Tanygrisiau

About the Area
Close to the heart of the great slate industrial areas of the Ffestiniog Valley, Tanygrisiau is a former quarrying/mining village tucked into the lower slopes of Moelwyn Mawr, not pretty but characterful, which is more than can be said for the modern commercial development in the adjacent valley bottom. From 1836 until World War II, the narrow gauge Ffestiniog Railway carried slate and (a little later) passengers from Blaenau Ffestiniog and the surrounding area down to the

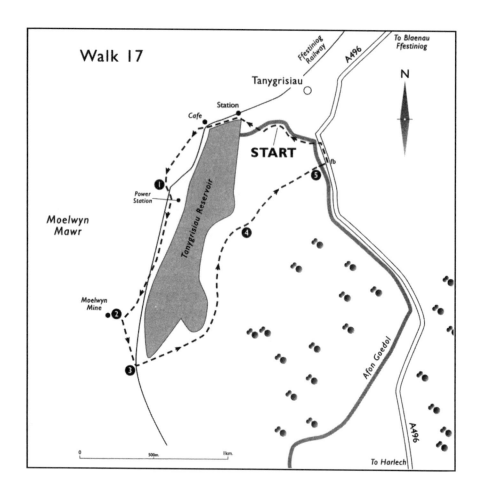

harbour at Porthmadog, the lifeline of the great local slate industry. Since the post-war restoration the railway has become a major visitor attraction.

High up the mountainside, the Stwlan Dam can be seen from near and far. This is the top end of the hydro-electric pumping scheme of the 1950's complemented by Tanygrisiau Reservoir and the power station which are at the heart of this walk. The centre at the power station and the high dam are operated as visitor attractions by First Hydro. Perhaps more importantly, construction of the reservoir cut the line of the then disused Ffestiniog railway. After long legal proceedings compensation was obtained by the railway company and incredible efforts were made by teams, largely of volunteers (the 'deviationists'), to re-route much of the line, including the spiral at Dduallt and the digging of a new tunnel. After several years work trains could once again reach Tanygrisiau and the old terminus at Blaenau Ffestiniog.

The Walk

Turn right out of the car park to walk towards Tanygrisiau railway station and the power station, crossing the outfall stream from the reservoir; Stwlan Dam can be seen, high up the mountainside. Pass the railway station, with a waterfall behind, then the cafe. Pass the access road to the power station, bearing right, then turning left at once at a footpath sign and field gate to continue along a rising surfaced road. Cross the railway line and pass a three-way signpost, with the forbidding cliffs of Moelwyn Bach to the right.

1. Leave the little road at a signposted left turn, downhill along a broad track, pass above the power station, go over a waymarked ladder stile, cross the railway line (ladder stiles on either side) and

Ffestiniog Railway at Tanygrisiau

Tanygrisiau

descend a rough track alongside the power station perimeter fence, passing a waymark en route to the reservoir shore. Continue along the track bed of the 'old' railway line, but turn right, uphill, at a waymark on a post, then left at another waymark just short of the railway embankment. Cross the line again, with stiles on either side, and follow the arrows. The distinct grass path rises a little above the line.

It is now very obvious why we (and the restorers of the railway) had to divert as the old trackbed can be seen disappearing into the water to head for the mouth of the old tunnel.

2. Pass the ruins of the buildings of the former Moelwyn Zinc Mine, bear right and climb a little hillside to a gap through a stone embankment, obviously the line of a former tramway, to reach a footbridge. Cross a tumbling stream and follow a terraced path across the hillside. Go through a waymarked gap in a wall and descend towards the line. Cross over, again with a ladder stile on each side, and bear left to start the return route.

3. Rise a little along a rough path, passing a waymark on a stone. Cross a more major track, continuing through heather, passing another waymark, this time on slate. Join a rough-surfaced cart track (waymark on boulder). There are more yellow arrows as a former

Tanygrisiau station

quarry is approached, forming a basin in the reservoir. The track goes beneath the sheer rock faces of the quarry, first up a rough little ascent and then turning left along the side of a protective fence, through heather and bracken. Shortly after leaving the fence, join a broader track and turn sharp right, uphill at first and then levelling to face the power station. Carry on to a fork; keep left here, then turn right to go to a ladder stile over a wall.

4. Walk up to a rock with the usual waymark, then join a wide cart track descending towards the main road, largely across wet ground, where walkers have obviously found their own diffuse routes.

   The views in this new direction include the least attractive part of Tanygrisiau – raise your eyes to the hills!

   A footbridge comes into view, ahead.

5. Cross the Afon Goedol on the bridge, go through a kissing gate and join the main road. Turn left along the roadside and, in a little more than 100 metres, turn left then left again to walk along the power station access road back to the car park, again crossing the Afon Goedol.

Walk 18: Dduallt and Tan-y-Bwlch

A short linear walk, generally close to the line of the Ffestiniog Railway, intended to be done in conjunction with the use of the train from Tan-y-Bwlch to Dduallt. However, for obvious geographical reasons, no footpath can follow close beside this railway line for long distances; the path does go up and down to a fair extent. The route is partially in woodland and partially in open country, with good views over the magnificent Ffestiniog Valley.

Distance	3½ km (2¼ miles)
Ascent	80m (263ft), half of this total being the approach to Tan-y-Bwlch. One or two steep ascents
Underfoot	Mostly good footpath but some sections are just a little rough. Three stiles
Maps	Ordnance Survey Explorer OL18, Harlech, Porthmadog and Bala, 1:25,000 Ordnance Survey Landranger 124, Dolgellau, 1:50,000
Start/Parking	At Tan-y-Bwlch station, grid reference 650416. Note – the approach to the station from B4410, heading north-west, is awkward. Leave A496 at the Oakley Arms
Refreshments	Station cafe at Tan-y-Bwlch

About the Area

Inevitably this walk is closely related to the Ffestiniog Railway and its history. Tan-y-Bwlch was for some years the terminus of the line as the post World War II restoration work was progressing length by length, and is still the principal intermediate station, with substantial facilities, including a cafe and shop. Later, Dduallt became the

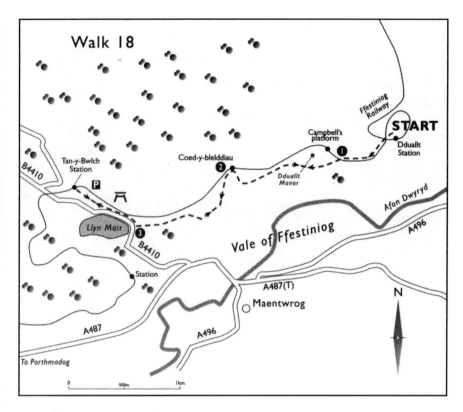

terminus of services for another long period whilst the 'deviationists' completed their magnificent engineering works on the spiral and a new tunnel, enabling services once again to work through to the historic terminus at Blaenau Ffestiniog.

The Walk

At Dduallt station, facing back towards Porthmadog and Tan-y-Bwlch, go over a ladder stile on the right to bear left along a grass path leading under the railway spiral. Bear right, angling away from the line, then go slightly left then right. Pass the end of a wall and continue to a gap in the next wall in less than 100 metres then along a good grass track, converging with the line.

The views over the Vale of Ffestiniog are superb.

Linda - a locomotive of the Ffestiniog Railway

1. Cross the line, with a ladder stile on each side, and turn right to descend, along a good path. Pass below Dduallt Manor (above is Campbell's Platform, for many years linked to the Manor by a ropeway), to a surfaced drive, then turn right immediately to follow a waymark, back up towards the railway line, through a field gate then over a stile in 20 metres. Continue, with Plas Tan-y-Bwlch now in view. Descend to cross a little valley, with a sleeper bridge over the stream. Ascend, at first at a reasonable gradient, then more steeply at the top, with a few rudimentary steps. The path rises and falls like a switchback for some distance, reaching the level of the line, with steps up and down. The route hereabouts, marked by orange splodges on the ground, goes through mature woodland.

2. Pass the tiny platform and cottage at Coed-y-Bleiddiau, built in 1860 to house a railway employee.

In the 1930's the cottage was rented as a holiday home by the eminent composer Sir Granville Bantock and, later, by H. St. John Philby, the father of the notorious spy, Kim Philby.

Descend to a footbridge over a stream and go up a few steps, with an impressive stone embankment on the right. The path remains high up the valley side, narrow but very clear, before descending to a fork. Go right here, to a little gate and then left through a coniferous plantation, with a stone wall on the left, descending then rising gently. Go through a little gate to join a more major track, over a cattle grid and descend steadily on this wide track, with a wall on the left, through mainly coniferous woodland, with plenty of larch and a few deciduous trees. The track leads directly to the public road, close to one end of Llyn Mair.

3. Turn right to walk along the quiet roadside as far as a small car park. From here the paths up through the National Nature Reserve are steep, rising directly to Tan-y-Bwlch station, with an ascent of about 40m (132ft). To return by walking along the roadside is more gentle but is obviously further.

If there is any doubt, send the fittest member of the party to collect the vehicle!).

To complete the walk, the direct route crosses a footbridge and continues up steps, joins a main track then goes up more steps before bending left to the top, still rising steeply. Go through a gap in the wall and keep rising to a gateway leading straight into the station car park

To the left are a picnic table and information board.

Walk 19: Abergwyngregyn

A really flat modest walk, linking the tiny village of Abergwyngregyn with a coastal nature reserve. Good views of Anglesey across Lavan Sands, Penmaenmawr and the inland mountains.

Distance	4km (2½ miles)
Ascent	Negligible, perhaps 25m (82ft) overall
Underfoot	A mixture of lanes and good tracks, with a short distance by the roadside and about 1km (²/₃ mile) along the back of the sand/shingle/crushed sea shell beach. No stiles
Maps	Ordnance Survey Explorer OL17, Snowdon and Conwy Valley, 1:25,000 Ordnance Survey Landranger 115, Snowdon, 1:50,000
Start/Parking	Roadside spaces, grid reference 656728
Refreshments	None

About the Area

If it were not for the Aber Falls, 3km (2 miles) upstream on the Afon Aber, few visitors would be likely to have heard of Abergwyngregyn and even less might have visited. In truth, there is not much to see in the village. Up the little road towards the falls, there is a car parking area 2km (1¹/₃ miles) short of the falls, which can be visited only by walking the remaining distance along a track rising steadily to a considerable height, perhaps a bit much for 'level' walkers.

There is plenty to see, however, at the coast. There are four nature reserves along the 9½ km (6 miles) expanse of Lavan Sands. Herons, golden eyes, widgeon, mergansers, oyster catchers, curlews, mallard and great crested grebes are just some of the array of waterfowl

Display board for nature reserves close to Abergwyngregyn

present in this area. The combination of inter-tidal habitats, sheltered sands, coastal fringe salt marsh, artificial brackish pools, with a freshwater input from two rivers, results in a great diversity of habitat.

The Walk

Set off along the road in the direction of Bangor, parallel with the main A55. Turn right in about 250 metres at a 'Conway' signpost to go under the main road. As this road climbs to the left to join the A55, turn right, along a minor road which soon becomes a country lane.

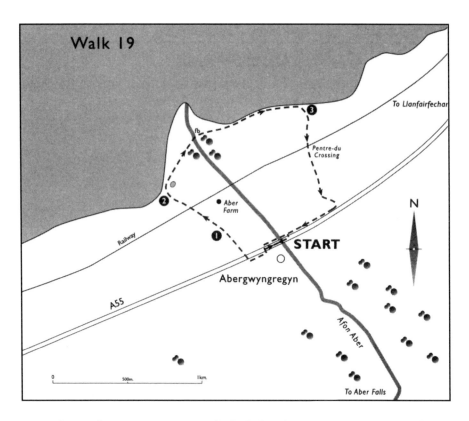

Walk 19

To Llanfairfechan

Pentre-du Crossing

Aber Farm

Railway

START

N

Abergwyngregyn

A55

Afon Aber

To Aber Falls

0   500m.   1km.

1. In less than 250 metres fork left along a more minor lane, signposted 'Nature Reserve', go under a railway bridge and continue to a footpath signpost by the Reserve's little car park, with information boards.

   The fine views are across Lavan Sands to Anglesey. There is a hide adjacent.

2. Turn right, through a kissing gate, then another, to follow a broad, track, with possibly a little mud in wet weather. Pass the edge of woodland and go over a footbridge crossing the swift-running Afon Aber.

   Ahead, Penmaenmawr, and the Great Orme beyond, are very impressive.

The route is now on the shoreline, with shingle and crushed shells underfoot.

3. Reach a stone wall and turn right, along a little grassy lane. Cross the railway line at a gated crossing and head for the main road (A55). There is a slight rise and the lane becomes surfaced, bending to the right to stay parallel with the main road. Cross the Afon Aber and turn left under the main road, then left again to return to the parking area.

Walk 20: Caernarfon

One of the longer walks, based on the fine historic town, passing through an attractive area, with wonderful views to the mountains and across the Menai Straits to Anglesey.

Distance	9½ km (6 miles)
Ascent	40m (132f), concentrated in the small area of comparatively high ground in the middle of this otherwise flat area. One short steep section on tarmac up to Ty'rallt Farm
Underfoot	A good mixture, including the Lon Eifion track close to the rejuvenated Welsh Highland Railway, very minor roads, lanes and the odd section of grass path, not always clear on the ground. Four stiles
Maps	Ordnance Survey Explorer 263 Anglesey East, 1:25,000 Ordnance Survey Landranger 115, Snowdon, 1:50,000
Start/Parking	Car park in Caernarfon, close to the castle, grid reference 479626. Alternatively, there is a car park at the public park/children's play area reached by the minor road to the golf club, south-west of the River Seiront, grid reference 474626
Refreshments	There is a wide choice in Caernarfon

About the Area

To the south-west of Caernarfon, the countryside is pleasantly agricultural, with a golf course and the added interest of the rejuvenation of the Welsh Highland Railway and the conversion of the trackbed of the former Caernarfon to Afon Wen railway into a trail for

Caernarfon Castle

walkers and cyclists, Lon Eifion.

The ancient town of Caernarfon nestles below the massive castle built by King Edward I in the 13th century as a major component in his coastal defences. The site of the investiture of Charles as Prince of Wales in 1969, it is now a busy visitor attraction in the care of Welsh Heritage. The town has ancient and interesting buildings in narrow streets and all the modern facilities to be expected of a thriving centre. A former small port, the mouth of the river is now used for pleasure boating, the small craft and the water much enhancing the views of the castle from the south.

The take-over of the former Welsh Highland Railway by the successful Ffestiniog Railway has resulted in a commitment to progressive restoration with through services to Portmadoc via Beddgelert.

The Walk

Leave the town car park close to the castle, with the river on the right, passing a roundabout before reaching the terminus of the Welsh Highland Railway.

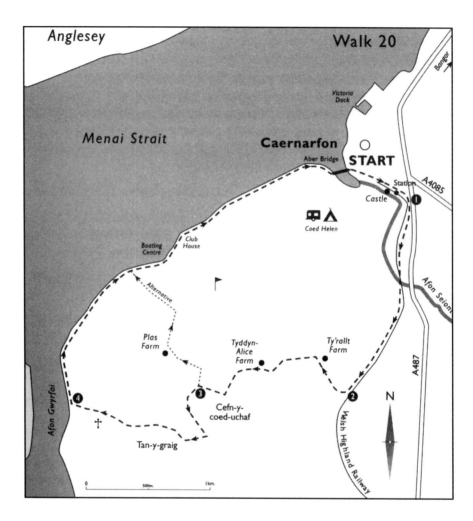

1. Continue along the roadside.

Look out for a plaque on the wall of a warehouse building on the right. This was the De Winton foundry where the relatively primitive locomotives which provided the earliest steam power in the quarries of North Wales were constructed.

In 150 metres leave the road to follow an organised walkway, Lon Eifion, with a symbolic bicycle on the overhead sign. Go under a bridge and continue along a well-made footpath/cycle way, rising slightly by the side of the railway line. Go under a modern bridge and cross the Afon Seiont on the railway bridge before going under another road bridge and into woodland.

2. Opposite a level crossing over the railway line turn right, downhill, through a gate with a 'public footpath' sign, to pass a garden centre. Go through a field gate, then another at the bottom, to reach a minor public road. Cross over, bearing slightly left to a 'public footpath' sign and follow a surfaced lane. The rise up to Ty'rallt Farm is the most significant of the whole walk. Go through a field gate at the top and along the right hand edge of a meadow. By a field gate/stile on the right in a few metres, turn left to cross a meadow diagonally, heading for a gate; the path is just about visible on the grass. Keep the same line across a second field to head for a gap in the hedge at the far boundary. By the third field, the path is even more obvious, bearing slightly left to a gate.

The views now include Snowdon and the heights of the Nantle ridge to the left, with the Menai Straits and Anglesey to the right.

Go through a kissing gate, with Tyddin Alice Farm in view, and cross the meadow to a waymarked gap in a hedge. Go straight ahead to a waymarked gate and turn right, along a farm access drive. At the farm keep to the left, going through two kissing gates in quick succession. Follow the line to the left, as indicated by a 'public footpath' sign, rising slightly towards the highest point of this upland area. Pass two old oak trees and turn left in 40 metres at a signposted kissing gate. Continue in the direction indicated by a signpost, passing gorse on the way to a field gate and a broad track past Cefn-y-coed-Uchaf. Bear right to follow the access track to a very minor public road.

3. At this road a right turn will give a shorter version of the walk, reaching the coastal road via Plas Farm.

For the full walk, turn left to rise gently and pass a former Methodist Chapel dated 1863, now beautifully converted to a dwelling. The road goes quite steeply downhill. At the bottom of the hill turn right at a 'footpath' sign, through a kissing gate, along a broad, level, farm track. 100 metres before Tan-y-Graig Farm, turn right, over a ladder stile with a white band waymark and ascend gently to follow the white posts across a meadow to another ladder stile. Keep to the same line to pass the farm, then head for the far left corner of the field, where there is a small gate. Continue along the edge of the next field, close to an old wall/hedge on the left. Go over a ladder stile, follow a farm track for 50 metres, then strike off to the left to head for an isolated church, passed to the right.

The church dedicated to St Baglan, appears to stand on a very old Christian site. Despite its isolation it is still consecrated and is occasionally used.

4. Join the road through a kissing gate and turn right.

This is a good road for walkers, plenty of roadside space, very little traffic and fine views.

The return to Caernarfon is about 3km (2 miles) in length. Unless the car park by the playground has been used, finish the walk in style by crossing the swing footbridge leading directly to the castle, then turning right to the car park.

Egwlys Pantheglan

Walk 21: Llanberis

A fine walk circumnavigating Llyn Padarn, based on Padarn Country Park which is situated on the opposite side of the lake from Llanberis village. Whilst the first quarter of the walk can hardly be called 'level', thereafter a steady descent is followed by a truly level return by the side of the lake. There are many fine viewpoints and interesting relics of the former great slate industry, making the initial effort well worthwhile.

Distance	8½ km (5¼ miles)
Ascent	Approximately 100m (328f), virtually all occurring in the first quarter of the walk - through Padarn Country Park. The track rises quite steeply, with 82 steps on the approach to the former quarry hospital
Underfoot	Mostly very good indeed – lanes, surfaced roads and good paths. Three stiles
Maps	Ordnance Survey Explorer OL17, Snowdon and Conwy Valley, 1:25,000 Ordnance Survey Landranger 115, Snowdon, 1:50,000
Start/Parking	Large pay and display car park adjacent to the Welsh Slate Museum and the Llanberis Lake Railway, grid reference 585604
Refreshments:	Cafe at slate museum; Cwm Derwen en route; selection of inns and cafes in Llanberis

About the Area

Llanberis has fair claim to be Snowdonia's best known village, sitting beside Llyn Padarn right at the foot of the great mountain itself, with the ever popular mountain railway providing a link with the summit for those who can't or don't want to walk uphill for almost 1000m (more than 3000ft). As a settlement entirely linked to the former slate industry, Llanberis can hardly be regarded as pretty but, with its shopping and other facilities, it does provide a good focal point for the busy tourist industry of the area.

The present day attractions within easy reach of the village include Dolbadarn Castle, Snowdon Mountain Railway, the very comprehensive Welsh Slate Museum, Electric Mountain, Llanberis Lake Railway and Padarn Country Park on which this walk is based. The latter includes a small museum in the former hospital.

The Walk

Walk to the far end of the car park, with a prominent incline visible on the hillside to the right and pass 'Padarn Lake Walk' and 'to the Quarry Hospital' signs to head towards the former quarry hospital.

In the car park there are several waymarked routes. Posts with a white band will be found throughout this route.

Llyn Padarn

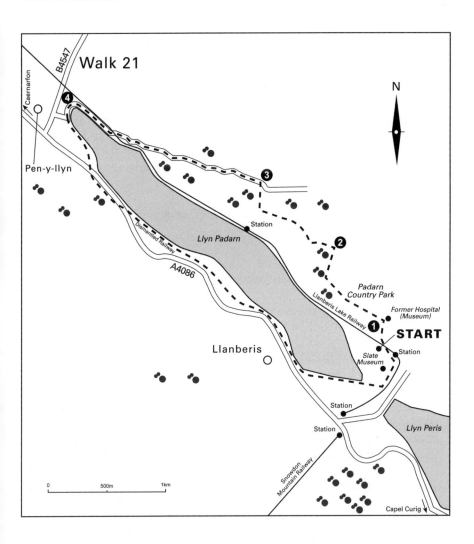

Follow a broad rising track, forking right in 20 metres to cross a footbridge and continue to the left, with the railway line below to the right and the view improving as progress is made. Pass a panorama display on slate and bear right to cross a bridge over the railway line.

If the flight of steps is too arduous, settle for a gentle meander using one or more of the various tracks around the car park.

Otherwise, onwards, up a total of 64 wooden and 18 slate steps in separated flights to reach the front of the former Quarrymen's Hospital.

1. Turn left across the front of the building to pass the detached former mortuary, dated 1906 and go through a waymarked gateway. A footpath now continues through woodland across a steep hillside, soon passing a real curiosity - the former outside toilet, with bench seating still in place. The path is still basically uphill but the gradients are reasonable.

A wayside bench is situated at a superb viewpoint.

The path eventually levels out, stony underfoot, but not difficult, then begins to descend after passing another bench; bear right to reach a waymarked kissing gate and a bridge over a stream.

The bridge is of great slabs of slate carried on old railway lines. To the right are attractive falls/rapids.

2. Rise up the far side of this little valley on a broad track, leaving the Country Park and passing under a former incline, down which trucks full of slate were lowered from workings high up the hillside to the railway line at the bottom. Pass above Cwm Derwen Woodland and Wildlife Centre and rise along the access track to a minor public road. A 'cut across' footpath saves a few metres but the gradient is, inevitably, steeper.

3. Turn left (there is yet another fine viewpoint a little way to the right) to follow this descending road for about 1½ km (1 mile) to the end of the lake, passing a few dwellings, some of them old, and through some woodland. Pass the terminus of the Llanberis Lake Railway and converge with the lake shore. Go left, then right, to cross the trackbed of the former Padarn Quarry main railway line of 1843 and reach the end of the lake.

The old road bridge (Pen-y-Llyn), nicely proportioned, is now in view.

4. Bear left to cross this bridge, passing an information board. After the bridge, turn left at once, along a disused road, passing the

Union Rock, a rallying point for disaffected quarrymen in 1874. Go over a ladder stile in 80 metres, then over a second ladder stile. Join the main road at a third ladder stile and, in less than 150 metres, go through a gap in the wall on the left to descend a slightly rough little path to join the trackbed of the former Llanberis to Carnarfon railway line, now promoted by the local authority as a route for walkers – Lon Peris.

This is a good level track along the lakeside, fringed with trees, bramble and gorse.

Pass a large pond, Llyn Tan-y-Pant, on the right, attractively rock-fringed and with swans in residence.

This water was cut off from the lake when the railway line was constructed.

Pass under a footbridge and then behind a recreation area, Y Glyn, on land jutting into the lake. Go through a gate; there are public conveniences on the right. Turn left for 10 metres, then right, along a pleasant woodland path; the white markers are much in evidence. Cross the access road to one of the recreation area car parks and continue. Join the recreation area access road, turning left to walk to the main road. Turn left along the generous roadside footpath. In about 250 metres, at the near end of a lay-by car park, fork left to follow a delightful lake shore path leading to a children's play area. Follow 'Padarn Country Park' at the signpost, bearing left towards the lake shore. Cross a footbridge, then another footbridge and a boardwalk, followed by a grass path. Go through an isolated kissing gate, and continue towards the slate museum. Cross a gated footbridge and walk past the museum to the car park.

Bridge at foot of Llyn Padarn

Walk 22: Pen-y-Pass and Llyn Llydaw

A rare and wonderful opportunity for 'level' walkers to enjoy the close proximity of high mountains, in fact the highest in England and Wales, walking with little effort at up to 440m (1444ft). Inevitably, this means out and back on the same track but the views are very different in each direction. On a fine day, with a picnic on the shore of Llyn Llydaw, this excursion is an alluring prospect, cradled in the great amphitheatre of Lliwedd, Snowdon and Crib Goch. For the more vigorous, a further kilometre along the shore of the lake can be walked before serious ascent commences.

Distance	5 km (3 miles)
Ascent	90m (295ft), all at easy gradients and mostly on the initial rise from the car park
Underfoot	Very good – the former Miners' Track, now a broad mountain walkers' classic high road to Snowdon. No stiles
Maps	Ordnance Survey Explorer OL 17, Snowdon and the Conwy Valley, 1:25,000. Ordnance Survey Landranger 115, Snowdon, 1:50,000
Start/Parking	Pen-y-pass at the summit of the A4086 Llanberis Pass – 359m (1178ft), grid reference 647557. Expensive. There are a few roadside pull off parking places nearby, likely to be filled early in the day. Park and ride bus service from close to Llanberis to alleviate parking congestion at Pen-y-pass
Refreshments:	Cafe at Pen-y-pass

The broad sweep of the Snowdon Horseshoe

About the Area

Snowdon is a great mountain, not only the highest in England and Wales, but also distinguished by its fine shape when viewed from almost any angle. Buttressed by substantial outliers such as Crib Goch, Lliwedd and Yr Aran, it has a substance and dignity which withstand even the onslaught of the hordes of people deposited at the summit by the railway from Llanberis and Hafod Eryri – Snowdon's new, £8.3 million, summit building – to which they resort. Obviously the ascent of Snowdon is beyond the scope of this book, but the suggested walk does allow admiration from below at comparatively close quarters.

Pen-y-pass is one of the great rallying points of mountain walkers' Britain. A youth hostel, a cafe and a car park now grace this highest

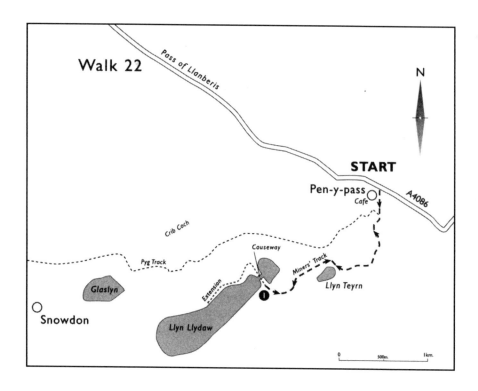

point of the Llanberis Pass, for generations the beginning of major routes of ascent - Snowdon on one side of the road, The Glyders on the other, taking advantage of the highest possible starting place.

The Walk

A broad easy track, pounded by the boots of walkers and climbers from time immemorial, leaves the back of the car park, through a gate. This is the Miners' Track, the first stage of the ascent of Snowdon. Detailed route directions are hardly necessary. Most of the total ascent comes in this first rise, at a reasonable gradient. On rounding a right hand bend, the sudden view of Snowdon, cradled in the arms of Lliwedd and Crib Goch, is magnificent. After the bend the track is basically level, with one gentle dip and rise. Close to Llyn Llyddaw go right at a fork to a causeway across the lake.

1. Turn round at the lake shore **or** cross the causeway and continue for a further 1km (²/₃ mile) along the far shore if a longer walk appeals. Return by the same route; Moel Siabod is now part of the extensive view ahead.

Walk 23: Abersoch

An enjoyable circular walk close to the sea, based on the delightful small town/big village of Abersoch, with lovely mountain views across the bay.

Distance	4½ km (2¾ miles) – 6¼ km (3¾ miles) with extension around headland
Ascent	A little more than 20m (66ft), plus 25m (82ft) if the extension is added
Underfoot	Very good throughout, paths, lanes and some minor road. No stiles
Maps	Ordnance Survey Explorer OL12, Lleyn Peninsular West, 1:25,000; Ordnance Survey Landranger 123, Lleyn Peninsular, 1:50,000
Start/Parking	Large free car park with public conveniences on the southern fringe of Abersoch, grid reference 314278. Look out for a left turn from the main road, signposted to the golf club
Refreshments:	To suit all tastes in Abersoch

About the Area

Beautifully situated on the east side of the Lleyn Peninsula, Abersoch is a comparatively quiet little place, most noted as a boating centre and for the views, a lovely combination of sea and mountain. From the village and its surrounding area Snowdon, Cnicht, the Moelwyns and Yr Eifles are all in view. The mountains behind Harlech, the Rhinogs, form a wonderful backdrop to the view over the wide bay. Although low key in its tourist attractions, Abersoch is quite pretty and does have a small museum and all the necessary shops and other facilities.

Abersoch harbour

The Walk

Leave the car park by walking along the surfaced roadway towards the golf club. Pass the club house and stay with this excellent track across the course as far as a major fork. Keep left here to head towards a small marina below the low headland of Penrhyn Du.

1. Leave the golf course and pass a few dwellings. 50 metres before a car park with public conveniences turn right to rise gently up a surfaced lane. In a little more than 100 metres turn right into a waymarked footpath, possibly a little muddy. Continue past a signpost, in 100 metres. The track soon widens, with a good surface, passing above a camping/caravan site.

The coastal views are magnificent.

108

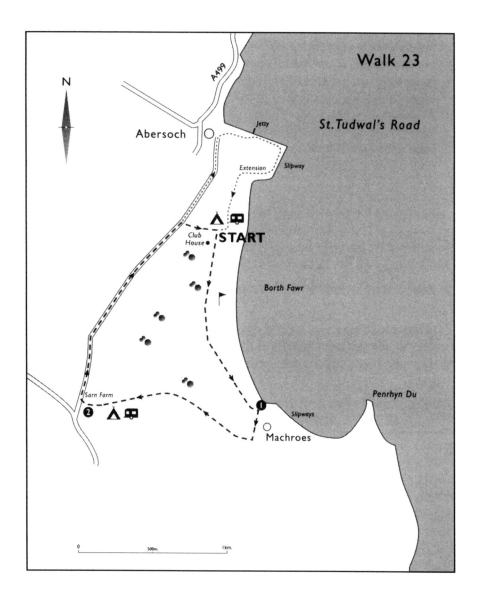

Reach a roadway which leads down to the sea, turning left then right to carry on, with the ubiquitous gorse and the hedgerows full of blossom in the spring. The track has only slight rise and fall throughout its length. After passing the top of a private driveway leading to a sewage works, as the roadway bends up to the left, continue straight on along a footpath. Go through two field gates to reach Sarn Farm, with its major crop of static and touring caravans.

2. Go through the farm to join the public road, turning right to return to Abersoch in 1½km (1 mile). An initial rise is followed by a long descent. Pass the Doctors' surgery and the fire station then turn right into the road signposted to beach and golf course to return to the car park.

To add the circuit of the headland, do not turn into the road back to the car park, but continue to the village centre, following the road as it bends to the right, above the beach, passing a comprehensive information board. Carry on along a rising cul-de-sac road and then go down a few steps on the left at a footpath sign. From the headland the views of Snowdon are particularly good. Go up a few steps to carry on round the end of the headland on a good path, with banks of gorse on the right. Quite suddenly, the two islands of St. Tudwal's, east and west, come into view. Pass a rough surfaced car park on the right; from this point a descent can be made to walk across the back of the beach, direct to the car park. Alternatively, you can bear to the right to reach a surfaced road and then turn left, gently downhill, passing public conveniences on the way to the main road. Turn left at the main road, then left again at the golf course road to return to the car park.

Walk 24: Morfa Nefyn

A circular walk from Morfa Nefyn, to the tip of Trwyn Porth Dinllaen (peninsula), then along a further stretch of this lovely, remote, coastline, with superb mountain and coastal views.

Distance	7¾ km (4¾ miles). Shorter version 6 km (3¾ miles)
Ascent	(full version) approximately 60m (197ft) in total, made up of several short sections
Underfoot	Mainly very good, a surfaced track to Porth Dinllaen hamlet, short grass on the edge of the golf course and fair paths on the return, but one awkward little descent at Aber Geirch (avoided by the short version). A little more than ½ km (¹/₃ mile) on public road at the end. Two stiles
Maps	Ordnance Survey Explorer OL12, Lleyn Peninsular West, 1:25,000; Ordnance Survey Landranger 123, Lleyn Peninsular, 1:50,000
Start/Parking	National Trust pay and display car park on fringe of Morfa Nefyn, by the side of the tiny road leading to Porth Dinllaen hamlet, accessed from B4412, grid reference 281407
Refreshments:	Inn at Porth Dinllaen hamlet and back of beach catering at Morfa Nefyn

About the Area

The great sandy sweep of the Porth Dinllean (bay) close to Morfa Nefyn is backed by low cliffs and a generally rocky foreshore. At the western extremity the peninsula forms a narrow protective arm, with a sporting golf course occupying most of the surface area. About half

Morfa Nefyn

way along are the remains of a pre-historic promontory fort. Tucked away by the beach below, Porth Dinllaen is a tiny place of great charm, well seen at long range from the recommended car park A little way further is a lifeboat station.

The village of Morfa Nefyn has no particular attraction, but is a useful minor centre for the area to the west of the larger Nefyn.

The Walk

Turn right from the car park and follow the 'Porth Dinllaen' signpost along the roadway towards the golf club. Pass the clubhouse and go through open gates to continue to a junction, where a short descent to the right leads to Porth Dinllaen, a remarkable little place, with inn and public conveniences.

If the descent and ascent do not appeal, the Porth can, of course, be bypassed.

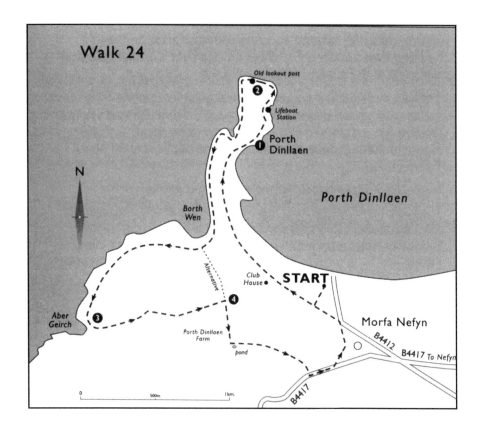

1. Carry on, briefly uphill, towards the disused coastal lookout post at the end of the peninsula, passing the lifeboat station nestling in a tiny cove, below to the right and then circling left to avoid an improbably sited golf course green and reach the lookout building.

2. Return along the west side of the peninsula, keeping between the golf course fairway and the sea, taking care to avoid golf players. In places, there is a distinct path on the ground. Bend round to the right, behind the bay, Porth Wen, to continue along the edge of the sea.

   For the short version, turn left in approximately 150 metres to follow a line of posts with white bands for 150 metres bearing left after the top post to a remnant of a stone wall and one upright stone which mark the end of a sunken lane. Follow this lane inland to rejoin the main route in 200 metres.

For the full walk continue for a further 1km ($^2/_3$ mile), sandwiched between the golf course and the sea, passing the occasional post with two white bands, until the rocky inlet of Aber Geirch is reached.

3. Beyond a golf tee go sharp left to follow a narrow path towards a shed. Before the shed bear right to a stile over a fence. The descent to the valley bottom is short and awkward. Many walkers obviously take avoiding action by keeping close to the fence on the left for a few metres, defying the close-packed gorse, and are then rewarded by an easy descent on grass. In either case do not cross the footbridge, but bear left along a wide, rising, track, perhaps a little muddy. As open grazing land is reached, stay close to the fence on the left to rise to a modern kissing gate. Go through and stay with the fence on the left, heading towards the golf clubhouse. Go over a ladder stile and turn right at the sunken lane beyond.

4. This old route, with a notable rabbit population among its gorse-clad banks, heads well to the left of Porth Dinllaen Farm. Go

Porth Dinllaen

through a gate and carry on to a swampy pond. Turn left along the farm access road, to reach the public road in about 1km ($^2/_3$ mile).

Morfa Nefyn village comes into view before the road is reached.

Turn left, then left again at the village fringe along a residential road signposted to 'Porth Dinllaen'. At the crossroads turn left to return to the car park in just over 100 metres.

Walk 25: Nantlle

An opportunity to explore one of Snowdonia's lesser known valleys and achieve a level walk quite close to the heart of this mountainous area. Not recommended during or just after seriously wet weather.

Distance	6½ km (4 miles)
Ascent	Approximately 50m (164 ft) in total. No prolonged or steep rise
Underfoot	A good deal of potentially wet and livestock-churned footpath. About half of the distance is along quiet, pleasant to walk, roads. Three stiles
Maps	Ordnance Survey Explorer OL17, Snowdon and the Conway Valley, 1:25,000 Ordnance Survey Landranger 115, Snowdon, 1:50,000
Start/Parking	As there is no car park in Nantlle village, park carefully by the roadside; outside the church is as good as anywhere, grid reference 511534
Refreshments:	Picnic only

About the Area

Formerly an extremely active slate quarrying area, the Nantlle Valley is now something of a backwater, quiet and with the former mighty quarries and their colossal waste heaps not particularly obtrusive. Altogether a pleasant place for a walk, with an attractive lake and a modest village. The Inigo Jones Slateworks, an all the year round visitor attraction, is not far from Nantlle, just to the south of Groeslon, by the A487.

The Nantlle ridge

The Walk

Walk along the roadside, heading west, soon leaving the village behind as the road bends to the left and Llyn Nantlle Uchaf comes into view. Stay with the road, with Snowdon visible through the 'jaws' of the low pass beyond the lake.

1. As the road bends to the right, turn left to go through a gateway and along a drive towards Fridd. Opposite the last building of the complex continue into a wide grass lane. Go through a waymarked field gate and a very old kissing gate in a further 30 metres. Join a broad agricultural track, potentially muddy. Pass a waymark, separated from the lake by a rush-covered wet area, cross a busy little stream and go over/through a ladder stile/field gate. Cross another little stream and continue beyond the end of the lake to head across a wide meadow to a distant ladder stile and field gate.

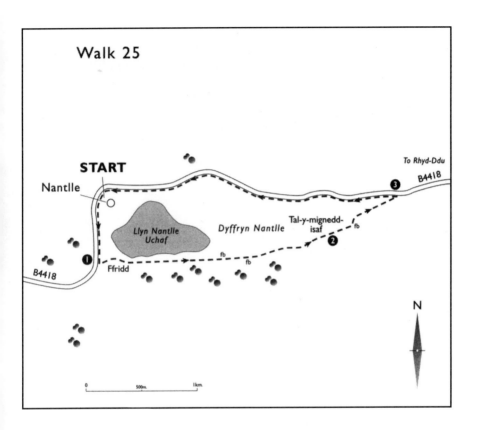

A course a little to the right of the straight line, leads to a bridge over a drainage ditch.

To the right are some of the peaks of the famed Nantlle Ridge, to the left cliffs guard the set back summit of Mynydd Mawr; in between is Snowdon.

Go over a ladder stile and cross a wooden bridge, then bear slightly right to another wooden bridge; streams really do come rushing off the hillside here. There are two field gates ahead; go through that on the left into a large meadow to head for a part ruinous agricultural building and join a farm trackway. Follow this to a field gate and on to Tal-y-Mignedd Isaf Farm.

2. Go through the farm and carry on up the farm access roadway, bearing left at a junction to cross a stream on a vehicular bridge, rising gently and crossing a cattle grid to join the public road.

3. Turn sharp left to walk along the roadside back to Nantlle, generally downhill, but with one or two slight rises, passing over a stream with a small waterfall and rapids. The distance is 3km (2 miles), the road is quiet and the views are good. Pass the village school before reaching your parking place.

Walk 26: Moelfre and Traeth Lligwy

A circular walk based on the attractive little seaside settlement of Moelfre, absolutely packed with interesting features and fine views, both close and distant.

Distance	6km (3¾ miles)
Ascent	Approximately 110m (361ft) in total. Small rises and falls along the coastal section and a more prolonged rise from Moelfre. No significantly steep ascents
Underfoot	Mostly very good. Mud possible at Pant-y-Gaseg and there are some rough and ready steps on the coastal section. Five stiles
Maps	Ordnance Survey Explorer 263, Anglesey East, 1:25,000; Ordnance Survey Landranger 114, Anglesey, 1:50,000
Start/Parking	Car park at Traeth Lligwy (pay), with public conveniences. Grid reference 496871
Refreshments	Moelfre Inn and cafe. Beach hut at Traeth Lligwy car park

About the Area

Moelfre is one of the most attractive places on the generally rocky north coast of Anglesey, occupying the south-east side of a small headland which provides shelter from the coldest winds. The unspoilt village has inns, cafes and shops and the Sea World Heritage Centre. The area is rich in pre-historic monuments, some of which can be visited on the line of this walk.

Traeth Lligwy is a fine sandy beach with a parking area, accessed by a very minor cul de sac road.

The Walk

Set off along a clear grass path on the seaward side of the beach building, heading for a signpost and rising slightly. The narrow path skirts the top of low coastal cliffs, with a series of excellent views, including Ynys Dulas, which has a low tower. The ups and downs include a few steps.

The wayside flowers include celandine, primroses, violets and wood anemones.

Go through a kissing gate then along the edge of a meadow to another kissing gate.

The Snowdonia mountains and the Great Orme soon come into view.

Turn left to another kissing gate and continue, with a wall on the left.

Burial chamber near Moelfre

1. Descend steps to a stony beach, Porth Forllwyd, cross a bridge over a little stream, and then rise up a few steps to a kissing gate giving access to a rather obtrusive static caravan site. Follow the waymark to the left, across the end of the caravan site to another gate and continue, the path becoming a little more rough. Go over an easy old stone stile, through a kissing gate to waymarks on a post.

Keeping to the left here stays close to the sea, joining the recommended route just above the pebble beach at the foot of the main street.

Bear right to a gap in a stone wall, to head for a waymarked gateway through the next wall. Go straight ahead across a small field to a kissing gate. Go left to join a surfaced road at a gate/stile; turn right at a 'village' sign to walk to a more important road in 50 metres. Turn right to join the main street in a further 50 metres.

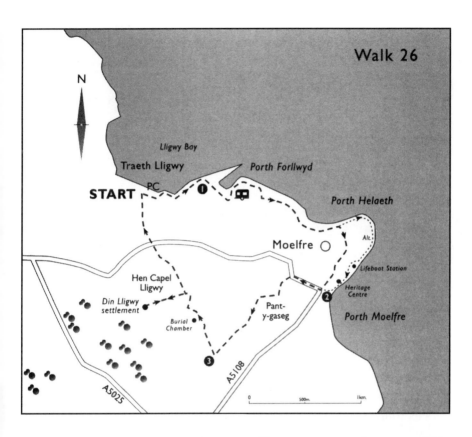

Turn left to descend past the post office en route to the tiny pebble beach. The Sea World visitor attraction is to the left.

2. Pass the beach and go uphill along the road. Turn right at the first junction, signposted 'Toilets', which are situated in a car park just to the left of the route. Continue along this residential road, uphill, to the splendid community centre. Turn left, to go along a concrete farm roadway, bearing right to reach Pant-y-Gaseg. Keep to the left of the buildings and turn left at a signpost to reach a waymarked stile. There may be churned mud here – stay close to the hedge on the right, bearing right to head for a waymarked stile. The next field has a distinct path to another stile, soon with a stream on the left. The path across the next two fields clings to the left hand edge, by the stream, before reaching a minor public road over a low stile.

Moelfre

3. Turn right to start back towards Traeth Lligwy, rising initially. In
    less than ½k (¹/₃ mile), turn left through a kissing gate to see a very
    fine burial chamber of 2500 to 2000 BC. Continue along the lane;
    just after a double bend a recommended detour to the fortified
    settlement of Din Lligwy starts at a kissing gate on the left.

    Go down the steps and keep close to the wall/fence on the left, then
    follow the Din Lligwy signs into the next field. Bear right, go through
    2 metal gates, enter woodland and climb a few steps to reach Din
    Lligwy. After visiting the village, follow the signs to Hen Capel
    Lligwy, a 12ᵗʰ century chapel with later additions.

    Return to the lane and go steadily downhill, crossing a more major
    road before reaching the car park.

Walk 27: Newborough and Llanddwyn Island

A most attractive walk through Newborough Forest and across the adjacent beach to and from the legendary island of Llanddwyn, rich in historic remains.

Distance	6km (3¾ miles)
Ascent	Approximately 50m (164ft) in total, assuming use of only the main tracks on the island. Variations to the east or the west can add considerably to this total. Apart from one short, sandy, slope, no steep ascents or descents
Underfoot	Good paths, forest tracks, and beach walking. No stiles
Maps	Ordnance Survey Explorer 263 Anglesey East, 1:25,000 Ordnance Survey Landranger 114, Anglesey, 1:50,000
Start/Parking	Large Forest Enterprises car park, with public conveniences, behind Llandwyn beach, grid reference 405634. Reached via Newborough village. A charge is made for vehicular entry to the forest
Refreshments	Picnic only

About the Area

Occupying the southern tip of the island, the former Newborough Warren has been extensively planted by the former Forestry Commission. Newborough Forest, primarily coniferous, now covers almost all the area between the village and the sea. Newborough

Newborough

village is a rather sprawling place almost 5km. (three miles) inland. Despite the visitor friendliness of Forest Enterprises and the provision of a large car park, this is still one of the quieter, off the beaten track, parts of Anglesey.

Once a true island, but now cut off from the mainland only at high tides, Llandwyn Island is a place of great character, rocky, sparsely vegetated and with a bleak remoteness unique in this area. Inevitably, such a place has relics of ancient occupation and a legend from the mists of Celtic Christianity. In the 5th century the locally based St Dwynwen, who is the Welsh patron saint of lovers, resisted attempted seduction (apparently not practising what she preached) by her friend, a Welsh prince. The couple parted in bitterness and in his sorrow the prince lived as a hermit (perhaps on Llandwyn?) for the rest of his life. In the interests of dull authenticity, it has to be pointed out that it is by no means certain that St. Dwynwen was, in fact, feminine. On a more prosaic note, there are pilots' houses, a lighthouse of reduced size, a commemorative cross and the ruins of an ancient church, all adding to the attraction of this fascinating place.

From the beginning of May to the end of September, dogs are not allowed on either the beach or Llanddwyn Island.

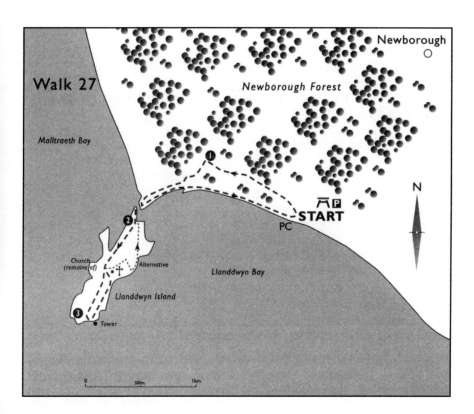

The Walk

From the public conveniences at the car park head towards the sea for 100 metres then turn right along a forest roadway, initially hard surfaced. Pass a vehicular barrier and an information board.

The forest hereabouts is mainly of Corsican pine on the sand dunes, a little monotonous but possibly welcome as a windbreak.

Ignore turnings to the right and continue to a 'T' junction.

1. Turn left towards the sea, bearing right at an open area to follow a vehicular track towards the beach. Just before reaching the beach, bear right, up and over a sandy bank, and carry on along a path just behind the beach. Pass a clearing with a seat before joining the

back of the beach, as the path becomes narrow and sandy. Bear right to head towards the now fully visible Llandwyn Island, hoping the tide is not against you.

The narrow gap, as the water surges from two directions, can be quite exciting.

2. Having gained the island, there is a fair choice of track. All are well used and are organised with yellow waymarks. For least ascent, stay with the broad 'central' track, rising gently behind the small shelter (and information) structure. For a circuit having the best of the wide ranging views, go right, up the steps, and stay close to the western shore. The various paths come together close to the church ruins and the prominent cross before continuing towards the lighthouse and the pilots' cottages, where there is a small exhibition and a gun formerly used to summon the crew of the lifeboat which was stationed here for many years.

An enclosure close to the church ruin may have a few of the unusual Soay sheep.

3. Set off back either by the main 'central' path or, if time and energy permit, by the path which loops around the slightly higher ground to the east, behind several charming little beaches. In either case, return to the shelter building and, assuming that there is no problem with the tide, cross back to the mainland at point 2.

Should you be marooned overnight on the island, you might have better luck with St. Dwynwen (or her ghost) than the poor old prince did; who wants to end up as a hermit anyway?

If you enjoy walking along the back of this fine beach, you can continue all the way to the car park, 1½ km (1 mile) distant. Bear round to the left at an obvious access track leading into the car park. Note that the further part of this beach route is not passable at high tide.

Otherwise, turn left to retrace the outward route through the forest or carry on further along the beach and turn left at the ramp leading directly to the 'open area' to retrace the forest route from there.

Walk 28: Llyn Alaw

Much more than a gentle stroll by an attractive lake, this is a comparatively long, demanding, walk, to be saved for a fine day and, ideally, combined with a lakeside picnic.

Distance	11½ km (7¼ miles). 13km (8 miles) to include the visitor centre
Ascent	70m (230ft) approximately, not in one continuous ascent. No steep gradients
Underfoot	A real mixture. Delightful lengths of footpath by the lake, but swampy sections in wet weather. Several fields without visible path
Maps	Ordnance Survey Explorer 262, Anglesey West, 1:25,000; Ordnance Survey Landranger 114, Anglesey, 1:50,000
Start/Parking	There are three possibilities. Recommended is the very small parking area, reached by turning from the Llantrisant to Llanabo and Rhosgoch road towards the visitor centre and then continuing along the approach road to the Welsh Water treatment plant, by-passing the visitor centre. At the near end of the treatment plant turn left along a track leading to a car park/picnic area in 50 metres, grid reference 377854
Refreshments	Picnic

About the Area

At 777 acres, Llyn Alaw is much the largest inland sheet of water on Anglesey, set among rolling farmland in the northern part of the island. The reservoir was created in 1966, by the construction of three dams. Now owned and managed by Welsh Water, it has settled down as an attractive lake, with leisure use by the public encouraged. Fishing, bird and other wildlife watching, walking and picnics, with an official visitor centre with toilets, all feature in the daily use. A hide has been provided and no less than 180 species of birds have been recorded. Selective grass cutting has encouraged the growth of traditional haymeadow flowers on the drier ground, whilst in damp areas, yellow irises, marsh marigolds and others may be found. Close to the visitor centre, a map of Wales, sculptured from rock and soil, is an interesting feature.

The Walk

From the recommended car park set off along a broad lakeside track, with the waterworks buildings above on the right and a pleasant little ecological area with a pond and bridge to the left. One of the smaller dams, below another car park, is soon reached.

1. Turn left to cross the dam and carry on along the lakeside, soon passing the first of the three rights of way which turn inland from the lake shore path; each is waymarked. From the dam, the distance to our turn off path is 4km (2½ miles) approximately. The path is not to be rushed, as it weaves in and out around inlets and to avoid patches of swamp, sometimes helped by a bridge or boardwalk, sometimes among trees, more often in the open. The second opportunity to turn right occurs about 1½ km (1 mile) from the dam. The first significant inlet needs care in route finding. Wet ground dictates a diversion to the right, towards a field gate. Do not go through, but turn left to keep as near to the fence on the right, as you must to avoid the swamp, and return towards the lake shore.

   Parys Mountain and its windmill are in view.

   Eventually, a post with waymark and a picnic table are reached.

2. Turn right through a field gate and along the left hand edge of a field to another field gate in 100 metres, followed by a possibly muddy lane. Pass a fishermen's rough car parking area by the buildings of Penworthyr Farm, now on a much improved surface,

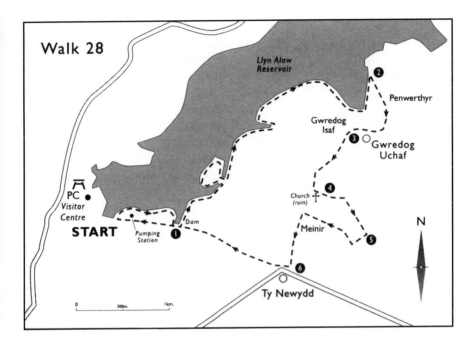

rising gently and then more steeply towards another farm. At a signposted junction with a surfaced road, turn right to pass through two adjacent farms, Gwredog Uchaf and Isaf, keeping right at a fork in front of a farmhouse.

3. Go over a stile beside a field gate and continue across a farm yard, through a field gate and along a good stony track, facing Holyhead Mountain, 15 miles away. In a few metres go left, through a waymarked field gate, staying close to the hedge bank on the left, rising to another waymarked field gate. Continue along the edge of the field towards yet another field gate but, 80 metres before that gate, go left, over a waymarked ladder stile, to head for a ruined church, Eglwys Adfeiliedig, noting the rather pathetic plaques still in place on an internal wall.

4. From the church, follow the direction indicated by the waymark to a modern kissing gate in the corner of the field, nearly 100 metres from the church. Cross a plank bridge and carry on with the hedge bank on the left to a former gateway, with a waymark

on a post. Bear right, uphill, at 45 degrees, across a large meadow, with Snowdonia now in view. Cross an intervening ditch on a rough bridge and go through a waymarked gap in the next boundary. Follow the indicated line across the next rising meadow to a stone-flanked former gate.

5. Turn right, along a wide grass trackway between old banks, soon turning right, uphill, towards Meinir, tucked away to the left, with Llanerchymedd village in view behind. Pass by Meinir, go through a gate, over a ladder stile, along a farm track, then through two field gates, before turning left at the first junction, soon reaching the public road at Ty Newydd.

6. Turn right, through a waymarked modern kissing gate and proceed across a rising meadow, staying close to the old wall on the right to reach a wooden bridge, boardwalk, and a waymarked stile. Continue along a large meadow, not straying more than 100 metres from the hedge on the right, aiming a little to the right of the now visible waterworks buildings, to a waymarked ladder stile. Go downhill, with a fence on the left, to a ladder stile/field gate at the

Llyn Alaw

bottom. Cross a lane, go over a waymarked stile and head for the waterworks buildings. Go over another waymarked stile to rejoin the lakeside path. Turn left to cross the small dam, go through a car parking area and follow the roadway behind the buildings to return to the car park.

Walk 29: Plas Newydd

Unlike many stately homes, Plas Newydd has extensive grounds which lend themselves to a walk of reasonable length, combining woodland and waterside in a very attractive manner, with the added interest of a great variety of plants, shrubs and trees introduced by a succession of owners of the estate. Unfortunately, only members of the National Trust or those prepared to pay the entrance fee for house and/or gardens can enjoy this walk, which is also subject to National Trust opening hours.

Distance	4½ km (2¾ miles)
Ascent	50m (164ft) spread over several short sections, some steep
Underfoot	First rate. No stiles
Maps	Ordnance Survey Explorer 263, Anglesey East, 1:25,000; Ordnance Survey Landranger 114, Anglesey, 1:50,000
Start/Parking	Official car park, grid reference 518698. Plas Newydd is reached from Menai Bridge and Llanfair P.G. by the A4080
Refreshments	National Trust tea room at entrance to property. Coffee shop at house

About the Area

With a delectable position on a south-east facing slope above the Menai Strait, Plas Newydd is an impressive 18th century house designed by James Wyatt. The views of the Menai Strait below and across to Snowdonia are magnificent. The house has an Italianate terrace and is surrounded by extensive landscaped grounds, including a celebrated rhododendron garden, started in 1937, reached at the far end of this walk (open only May-June). Most of the earlier garden

The Britannia Bridge over the Menai Strait

landscaping was carried out by Humphry Repton, leading landscape improver of his day, at the end of the 18th century. On the large grass area between the entrance building and the large former stables block, stands a rather forlorn part collapsed Neolithic burial chamber, long shorn of its overlay of soil, known as the Cromlech. Weather and tides permitting, boats trips on the Strait are operated from a quay below the house.

Inside, an exhibition of the work of Whistler includes his largest painting. There is also a military exhibition which includes relics of the Battle of Waterloo.

The property is subject to the normal National Trust opening season, generally April to October inclusive, with closure on Thursdays and Fridays. The tea room is open Friday, Saturday and Sunday during November and most of December. There is a reduced entrance fee for garden and grounds only.

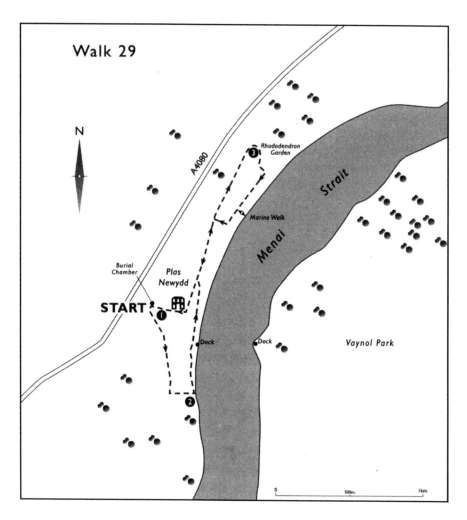

The Walk
Pass through the shop and the ticket office, with the tea room adjacent, formerly the dairy, and continue along the track, passing large old conifers and a shelter belt of *Cupressus macrocarpa*. The line of the former ha ha is nearby.

1. Turn right at the first junction, already enjoying the fine views which are such a feature of this walk. Bear left from the track before a 'private' sign is reached to walk along a broad grass path

through the arboretum, which includes plants of Australian origin among its many varieties. Leave the arboretum by joining a surfaced track. Turn right; in 15 metres turn left at a junction to head downhill in a straight line towards the water. At the bottom is a fine waterside viewpoint from which a first view of the Britannia Bridge, now carrying both road and rail, and also the column erected in 1817 in honour of the 1st Marquis of Anglesey, to which a bronze statue was added in 1860, six years after the death of the Marquis.

2. Carry on along the track towards the house. Reach a more major roadway and go straight across to a narrow footpath descending via steps to a waterside terrace. To the right is a dock, nothing to do with the National Trust. Continue below the house, passing cannons and the landing stage from which boat trips are operated. Go up steps at the far end to follow a stony trail, soon joining a more major track. Turn right, still rising through woodland. Pass a large building used as a sea cadet training centre and, at a 'private' sign across the track and a post with green (woodland) and blue (marine) walk waymarks, descend towards the shore, turning left at a junction to follow a 'Rhododendron Garden' sign.

In Spring the woodland is rich in daffodils, bluebells, primroses and wood anemones.

Stay with this path for the full distance to the Rhododendron Garden, open only from April to June, crossing the occasional stream.

3. Turn round to return, soon turning left at a waymarked post to go down a narrower track towards the water, then follow the 'Marine Walk', which is an entirely delightful footpath, just above the water's edge. Turn right, up stone steps, to rejoin the outward track at a waymark, turning left at the junction for a short distance before a right turn brings you once more to the main track ('Lady Uxbridge's Walk'). Turn left to walk to the house; the terrace garden is above on the right. Pass the front of the house; turn right at the end of the house. Turn right again for a few metres before going to the left, up steps and a rising path, to rejoin the outward route and return, via the shop, to the car park.

Walk 30: Cemlyn Bay

A varied circuit including some very attractive coastline, a historic mining area, pleasant countryside and the important Cemlyn Bay Nature Reserve.

About the Area

The peaceful area around Cemlyn Bay has a distinctly remote feel, that 'Celtic fringe' which is common to many extreme westerly parts of the British coastline. Bryn Aber was a tiny fortress-like building constructed on these ancient rocks long before the North Wales Wildlife Trust developed their reserve at the back of the bay, adding a weir (rebuilt in 1978) to the natural ridge of shingle to enclose a large pool of brackish water. The array of waterfowl to be seen here is staggering, summer visitors including terns, sea swallows, mallard, shelduck, redshanks, oystercatchers, red breasted merganser and coots, whilst a whole array of the duck family take winter refuge. Likewise, the coastal vegetation is rich and varied.

Distance	7½ km (4¾ miles). 8½ km (5¼ miles) with extension
Ascent	75m (246ft) in total, well-spaced and without steep gradients. The extension adds about 20m (66ft) to this total
Underfoot	Some fine footpaths, short-cropped grass and about 1½ km (1 mile) of minor road. Eight stiles
Maps	Ordnance Survey Explorer 262, Anglesey West, 1:25,000; Ordnance Survey Landranger 114, Anglesey, 1:50,000
Start/Parking	Spacious free car park close to Bryn Aber, accessed by a narrow lane. Leave the A5025 at Tregele; turn right at the side of the lagoon, grid reference 329937
Refreshments	Picnic only

Cemlyn Bay

In complete contrast, a short distance along the coast Wylfa Power Station has a visitor centre.

The Walk

Start from the end of the car park by heading towards the sea along a stony lane. Go through a gate and walk to a simple monument marking 150 years (1828-1978) since the launching of the first lifeboat on Anglesey.

Unfortunately the view along the coast to the right is dominated by the huge bulk of Wylfa Power Station.

1. In a few metres further, turn left along a grass path, then turn left again, through a gate, to follow a grass path, rising above the shoreline.

   Rocky islets in view (one with lighthouse) include the Skerries.

   Go through a kissing gate, then a second kissing gate.

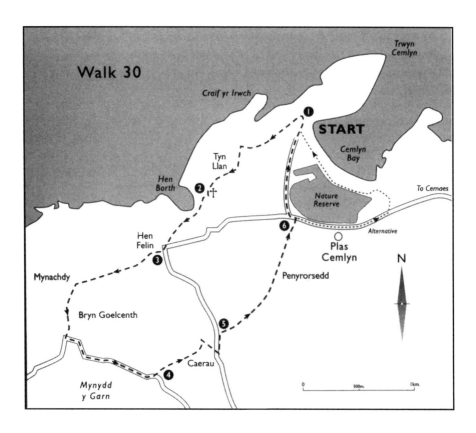

To the left Mynydd y Garn hilltop – 170m (558ft) is crowned by a monument.

Go through a fourth kissing gate and turn inland just before a field gate, along a farm track with a ditch and a fence on the right, heading a little left of Tyn Llan Farm. Go through a field gate and turn right to pass through the farm and over a ladder stile, reaching an isolated church in less than 200 metres.

2. To continue on the coast path pass round the back of the church to another ladder stile, with route finding helped by various signs. Carry on beside a wall, then bear right to a stile/gate and walk across the back of Hen Borth shingle beach for 100 metres. Turn left through a kissing gate, then left again through another kissing

gate to leave the coast path. Head towards the visible roof of Hen Felin, with a fence and a stream close on the left. In 150 metres go through a kissing gate, cross a bridge over a stream and pass a National Trust board with information about the historic Mynachdy mining area, the nearby Roman lookout post, the Skerries lighthouse of 1713, and 19th century ruins. Go through a little gate to join a surfaced road, where there are signposts.

3. Go over a stone stile beside Hen Felin entrance gate, pass to the right of the house and up a grass lane to a ladder stile on the left. Bear right along a path which is just about visible on short grass to a waymarked gate/stile. A farm track now heads towards the large farmstead of Mynachdy; above, to the right, are substantial industrial ruins. At the farm take the third gate on the left to follow the concrete access road, gently uphill, passing Bryn Goelcerth and continue to rise on what is now a very minor road. Turn left at a junction (the highest point of the walk, almost 45m.- 148ft.). Carry on along this quiet lane, below Mynydd y Garn, passing a few properties. Go straight ahead at a road junction.

4. In a further 60 metres turn left at a kissing gate to follow the line of a low embankment of earth and stone, over short cropped grass to a kissing gate at the far end. Go diagonally across the next field to a kissing gate, then approach a large farmstead along a grass lane. Go past the farm buildings and house to a metal gate.

   There are many very old, probably historic, buildings here – 'Caerau' on the Ordnance Survey map.

   At an abandoned pair of cottages, Fron Hendry, turn right to walk to the public road in a little more than 100 metres Turn left to reach a signposted kissing gate in 50 metres.

5. Turn right here, to rise along the edge of a meadow, with a wall on the left and some nice rock outcrops. Continue through a gate, with the wall still on the left, to a kissing gate. The huge farm complex of Penyrorsedd is to the right, ahead. Approach a field gate, but go over a stile 20 metres to the right of the gate, staying with the wall. Go through another kissing gate, pass the farm buildings, and head for a stile, over possibly cattle-churned ground. Go up a slight rise

to a modern kissing gate close to the house, Bwthyn Penreos. Pass the house, with lovely views over the Nature Reserve, to descend the tarmac entrance drive, fringed with a selection of garden shrubs and daffodils, to a stile giving access to the public road, beside the water.

6. **For a small extension to the route and a circuit of the Nature Reserve** turn right, along the road, uphill for nearly 1km ($^2/_3$ mile), passing Plas Cemlyn on the way. Turn left at a road junction to descend to a car park, then turn left to walk along the shingle bank to return to our car park. Note – in the waterfowl breeding season visitors may be requested to keep off the shingle bank. Note (2) – at high tide it may be necessary to paddle across the outflow from the lagoon.

For the direct return, turn left along the road, then right in 40 metres to walk along the access roadway to Bryn Aber and the car park

Also available from Sigma

HOLIDAY WALKS IN NORTH WALES
Brian Conduit

20 walks ranging from 2 to 6 miles in length, all within the capabilities of most people, varying in difficulty and the nature of the terrain. The scenery is varied and magnificent and the walks vary from easy and flat riverside strolls to more challenging walks in the Snowdonia National Park or on the slopes of the Clwydian hills.
£8.99

ALL-TERRAIN PUSHCHAIR WALKS: SNOWDONIA
Zoë Sayer & Rebecca Terry

A superb collection of pushchair-friendly walks for North Wales. These 30 routes explore the spectacular scenery of the Snowdonia National Park – including an adventurous walk that takes you and a pushchair half-way up Snowdon! The walks range from simple riverside strolls to full-on alpine-style stomps.
£7.95

PEMBROKESHIRE WALKING ON THE LEVEL

Norman & June Buckley

This is the sixth volume of the popular and well-establsihed series of 'level walks' books. Discover both the breath-taking splendour of the Pembrokeshire coast and its diverse inland landscape. The 25 comparatively short, easy walks in this book include clear route directions, map and a brief description of features encountered along the way as well as recommendations for refreshment. £8.99

ALL-TERRAIN PUSHCHAIR WALKS: ANGLESEY & LLEYN PENINSULA

Zoë Sayer & Rebecca Terry

Pushchair walks by the sea — from beach strolls to cliff-top rambles. There are 30 tried-and-tested routes from simple beach strolls to rugged inland hill-top rambles through fields, woods and over hills and mountains with scarcely any obstacles and never any need to remove the child from the pushchair. £7.95

WALKS IN THE FOREST OF DEAN AND WYE VALLEY
Dave Meredith

The Forest of Dean and Wye Valley is a paradise for both the keen rambler and the casual stroller. The 22 walks described in this book are along easy footpaths taking you to spectacular viewpoints, along woodland glades carpeted with bluebells, daffodils and foxgloves, and under the dappled shade of its golden autumn canopy. £8.99

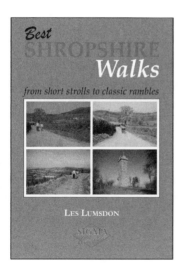

BEST SHROPSHIRE WALKS 2ND EDITION
From short strolls to classic rambles
Les Lumsdon

A new revised edition of this much loved guide contains 36 walks, including 12 completely new routes, located in all parts of the county. Several walks feature fine hill walking on the Welsh borders and others start from delightful villages and hamlets in the north and east of the county.

The Shropshire countryside really comes alive in this well-researched book. All of the walks include stories about the locality: folklore and legends, attractions and facilities. There are clear maps and a selection of photographs to make for an enjoyable and informative read.
£8.99

PEAK DISTRICT WALKING
On The Level
Norman Buckley

This is a book for people who enjoy a relaxed approach to walking — walks that can be enjoyed whatever the weather. The walks are ideal for family outings and the precise instructions ensure that there is little chance of losing your way. Well produced maps and inviting photographs encourage everyone to try out the walks.

The whole of the Peak District is covered — both the Dark Peak and the White Peak — with visits to such gems as Edale, Castleton, Eyam, Chatsworth and Bakewell.
£7.95

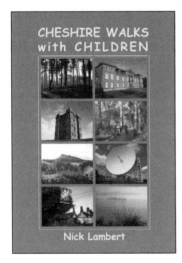

CHESHIRE WALKS WITH CHILDREN
2nd Edition
Nick Lambert

Now completely revised and updated, this was the first in our "walks with children" series and has quickly become a firm favourite. There are 30 walks, ranging in length, together with things to look out for and questions to answer along the way make it an entertaining book for young and old alike.
£8.99